Fairyland
CHRISTMAS BY SIMI

SIMI RAGHAVAN

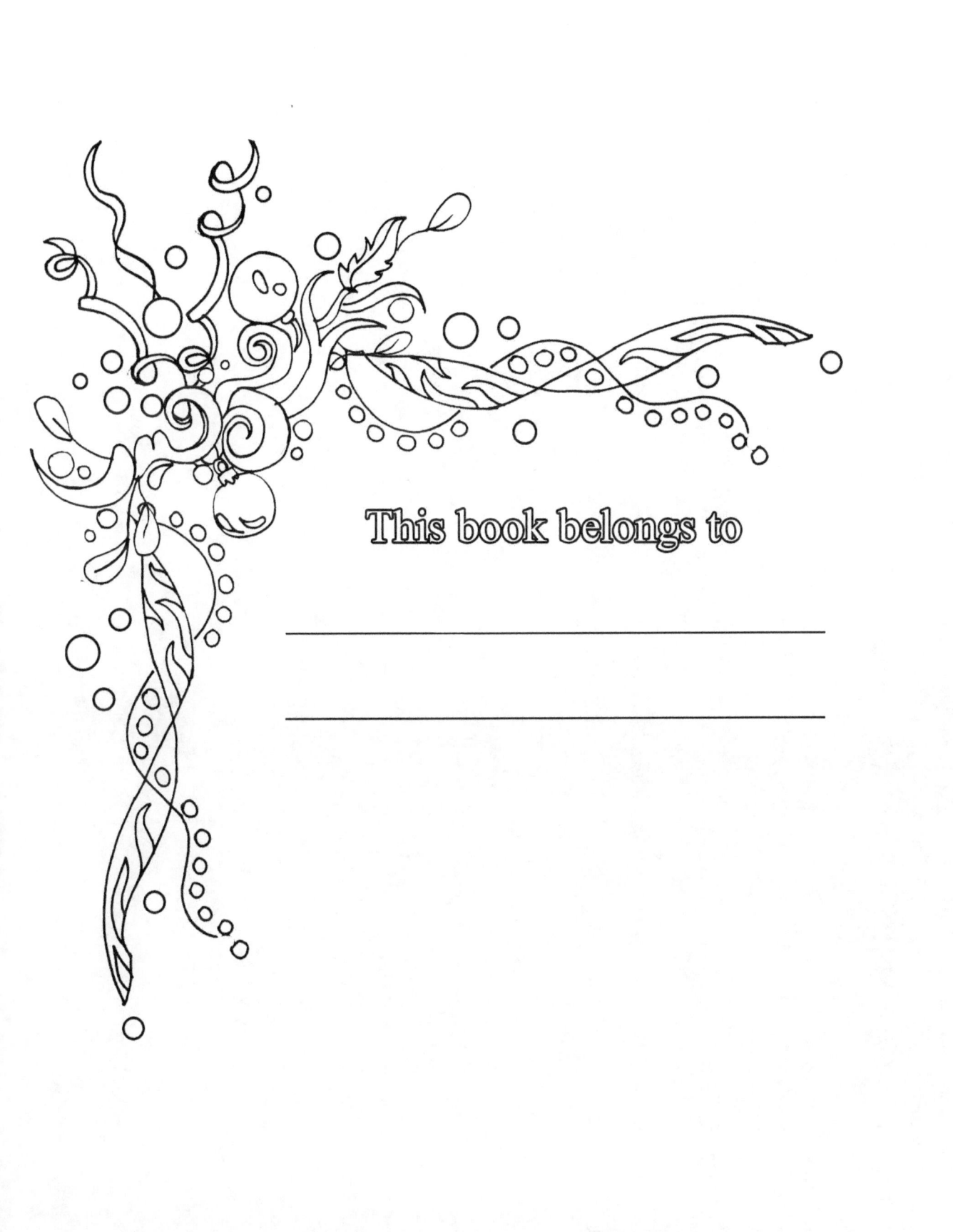

This book belongs to

_____

_____

ISBN-13: 978-1534995420
ISBN-10: 1534995420

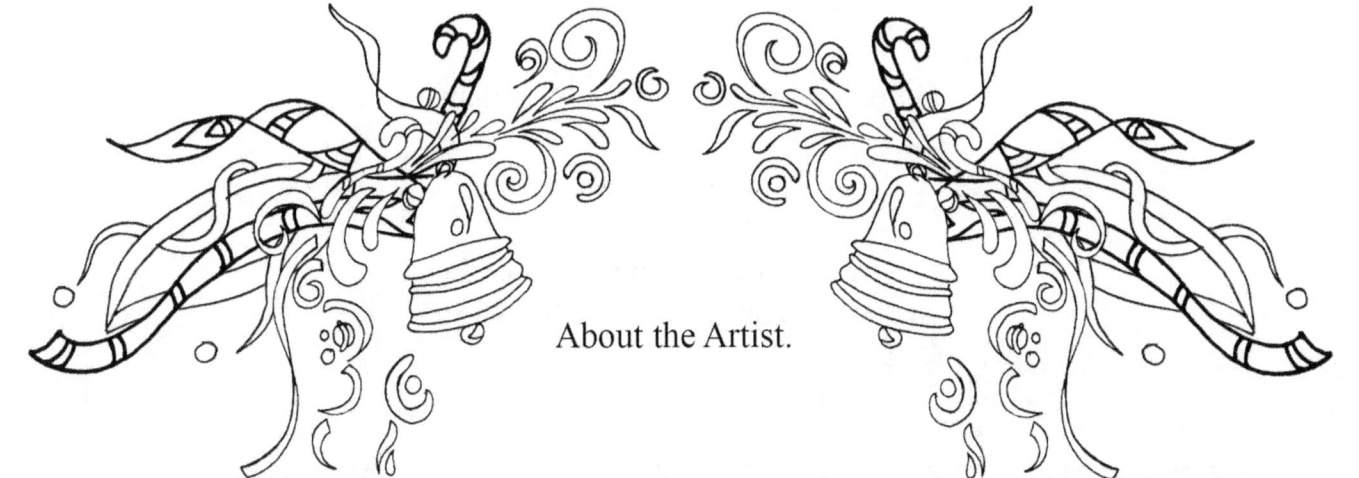

About the Artist.

Simi lives in the exotic land of Kerala, in India with two kids who bug her the whole day, one super-excited-for-just-about-anything dog & a loving,caring husband (He will be reading this;)).She loves sketching & when she manages to get some artwork saved from the evil clutches of her 3year old, she turns them into awesome coloring books for you. Have fun coloring, leave a review on amazon & don't forget to post your colored pages on her facebook group. Happy coloring :)

www.simiraghavan.com
www.amazon.com/author/simiraghavan
www.facebook.com/simiraghavanart
www.facebook.com/groups/simiraghavan
simiraghavanart@gmail.com

"Christmas is my favourite holiday & I am one of those people who put up the christmas tree in October. I had great fun creating the artwork in this book & I'm sure you will have fun coloring them too. I have seen amazing versions of the colored pieces of my pages from the Halloween book & would love to see the same from my christmas pages too. Do share your work on my fb group!"
 -Simi.

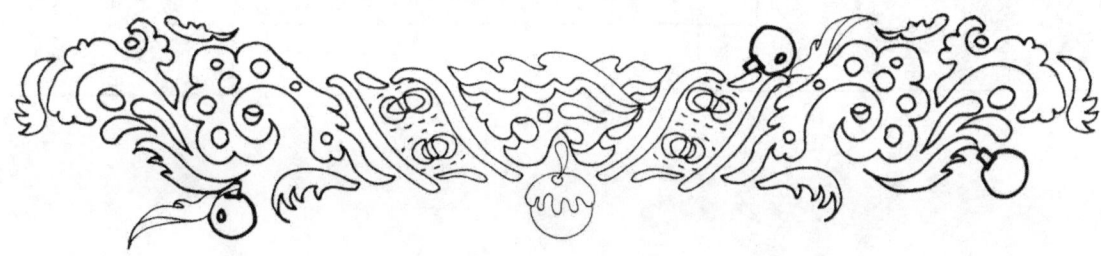

Other books by Artist Simi Raghavan:

Halloween by Simi
Available on:
www.amazon.com/dp/1537508563/
www.amazon.co.uk/dp/1537508563/

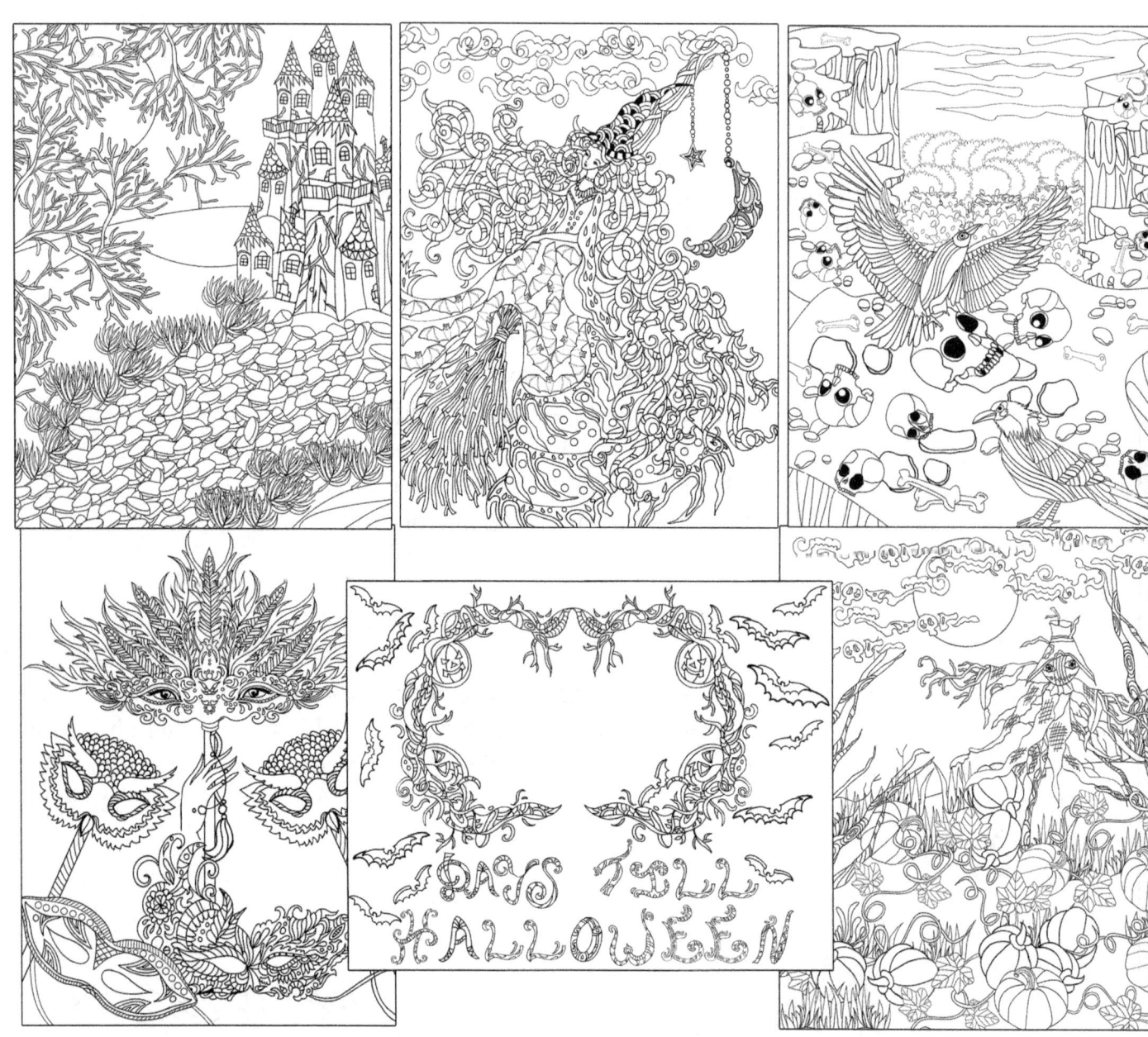

Contents

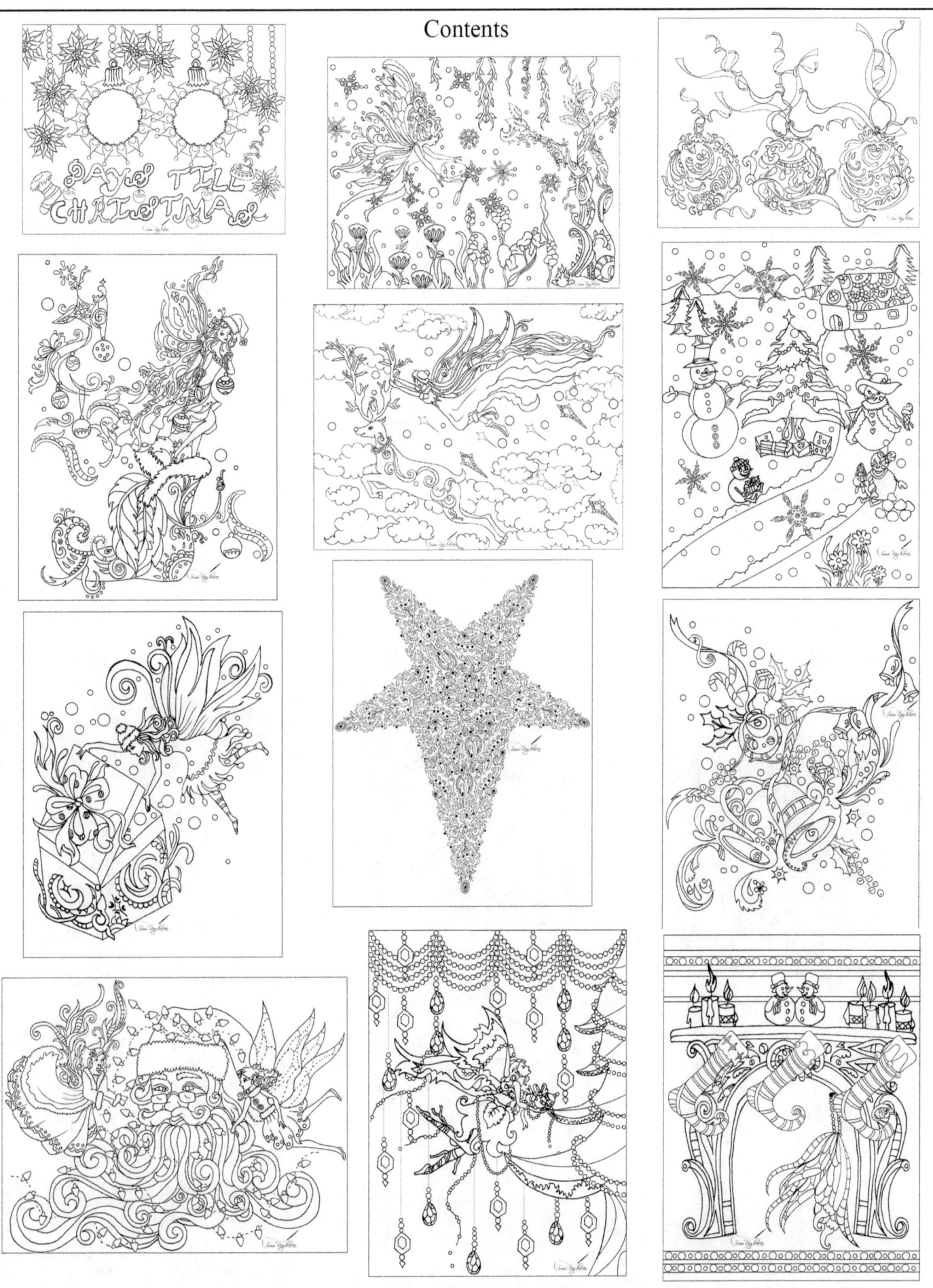

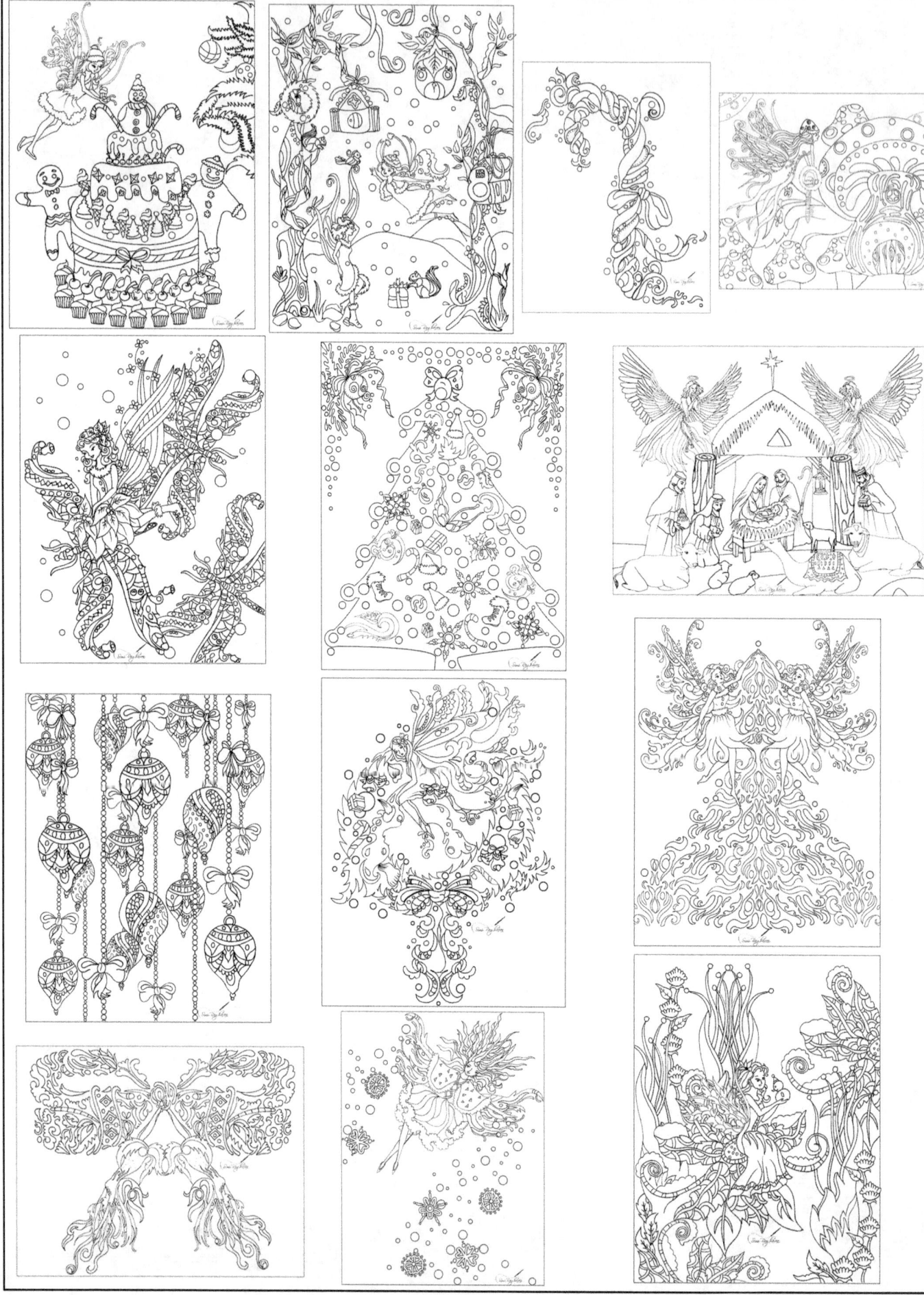

Feel free to test out your colors here.

Use sticky notes to stick on numbers inside the baubles for the Christmas countdown page.

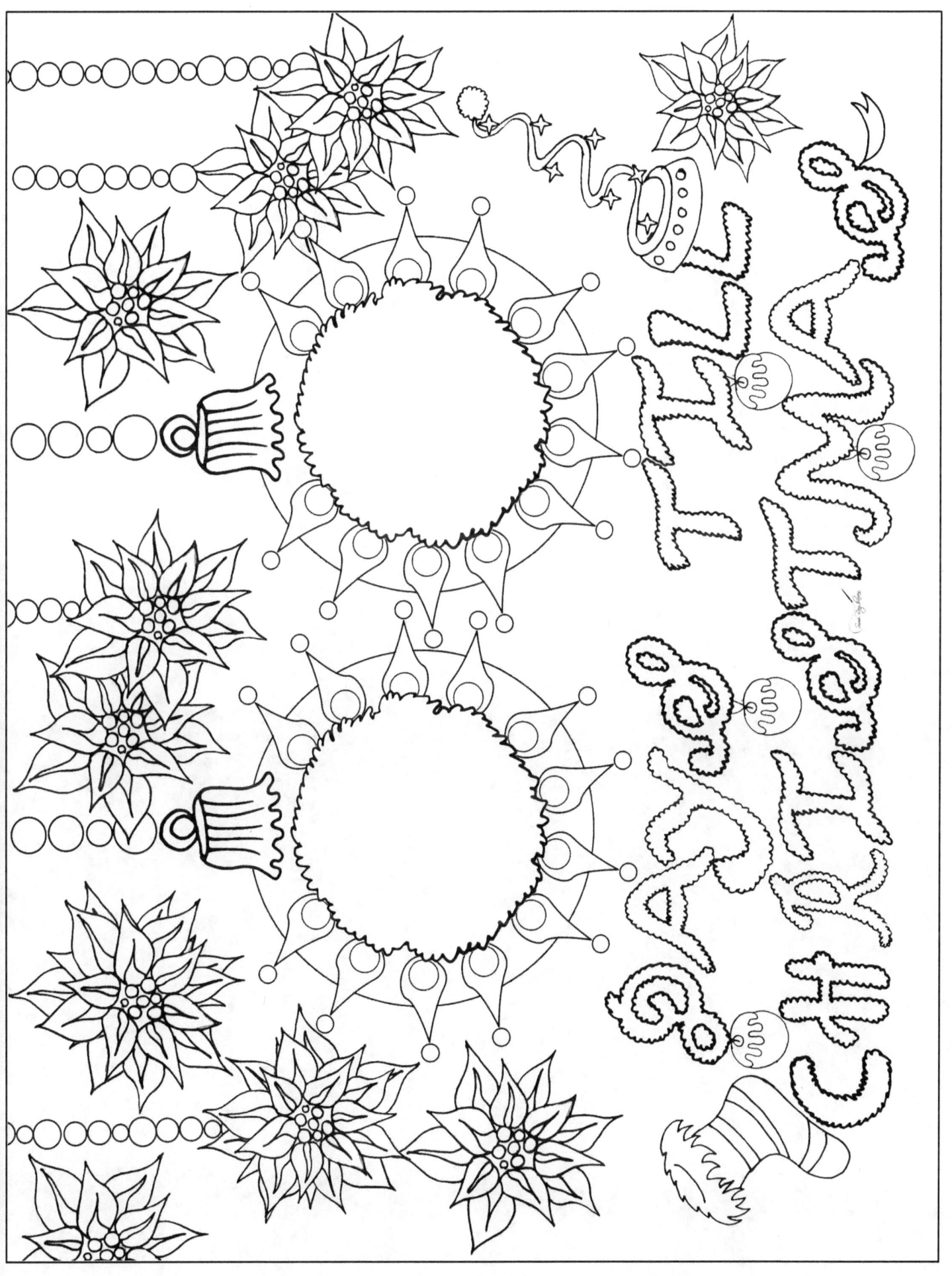

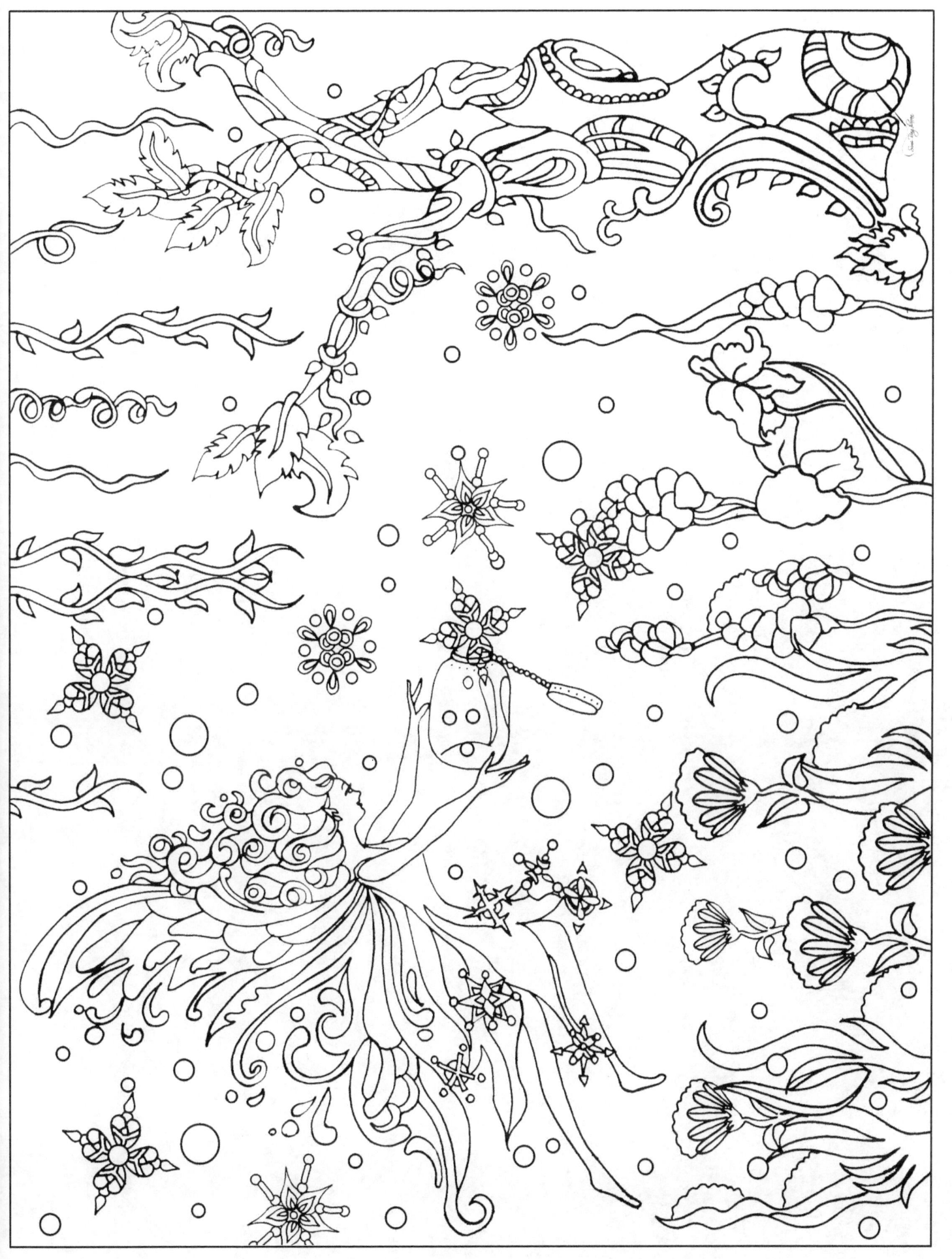

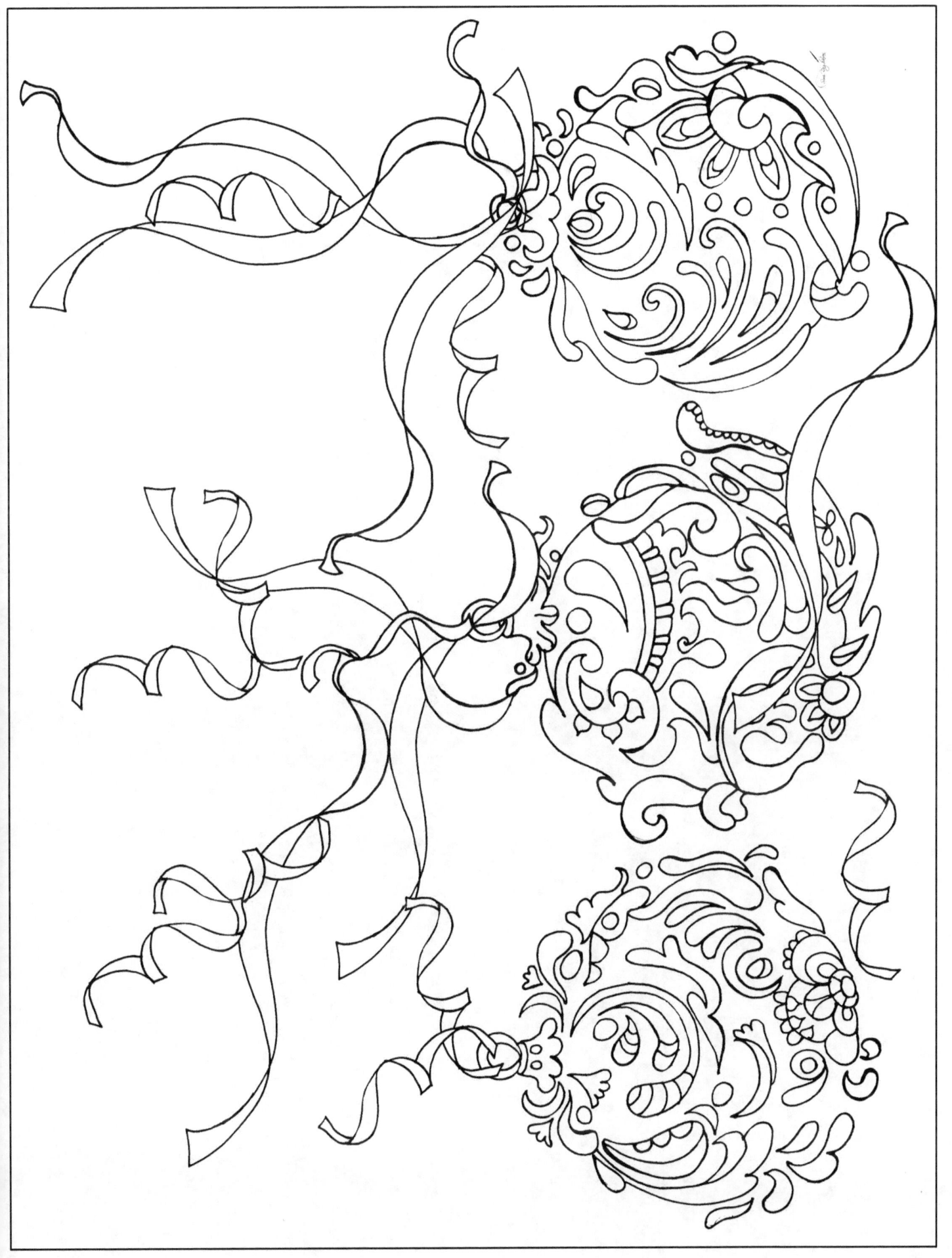

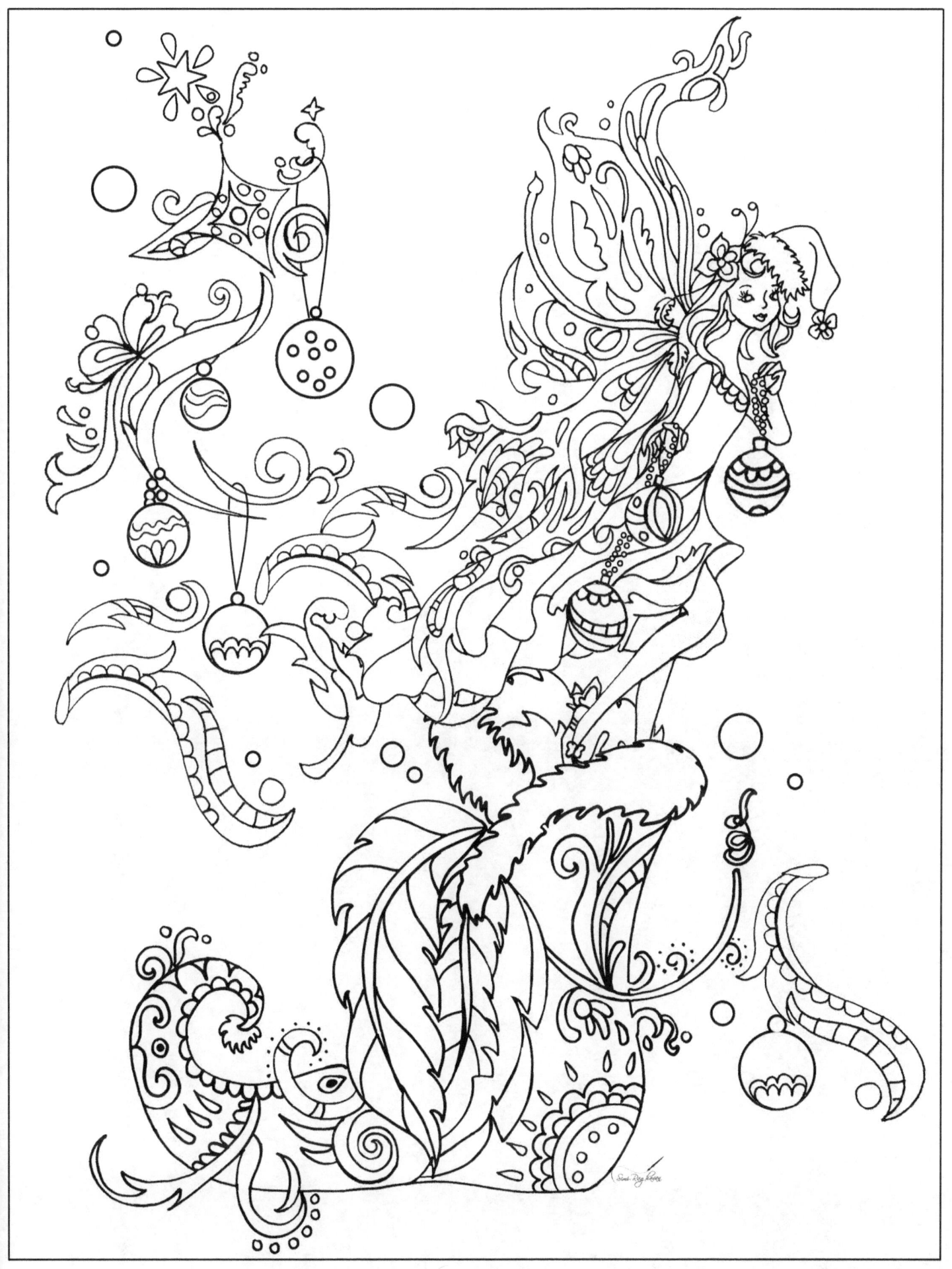

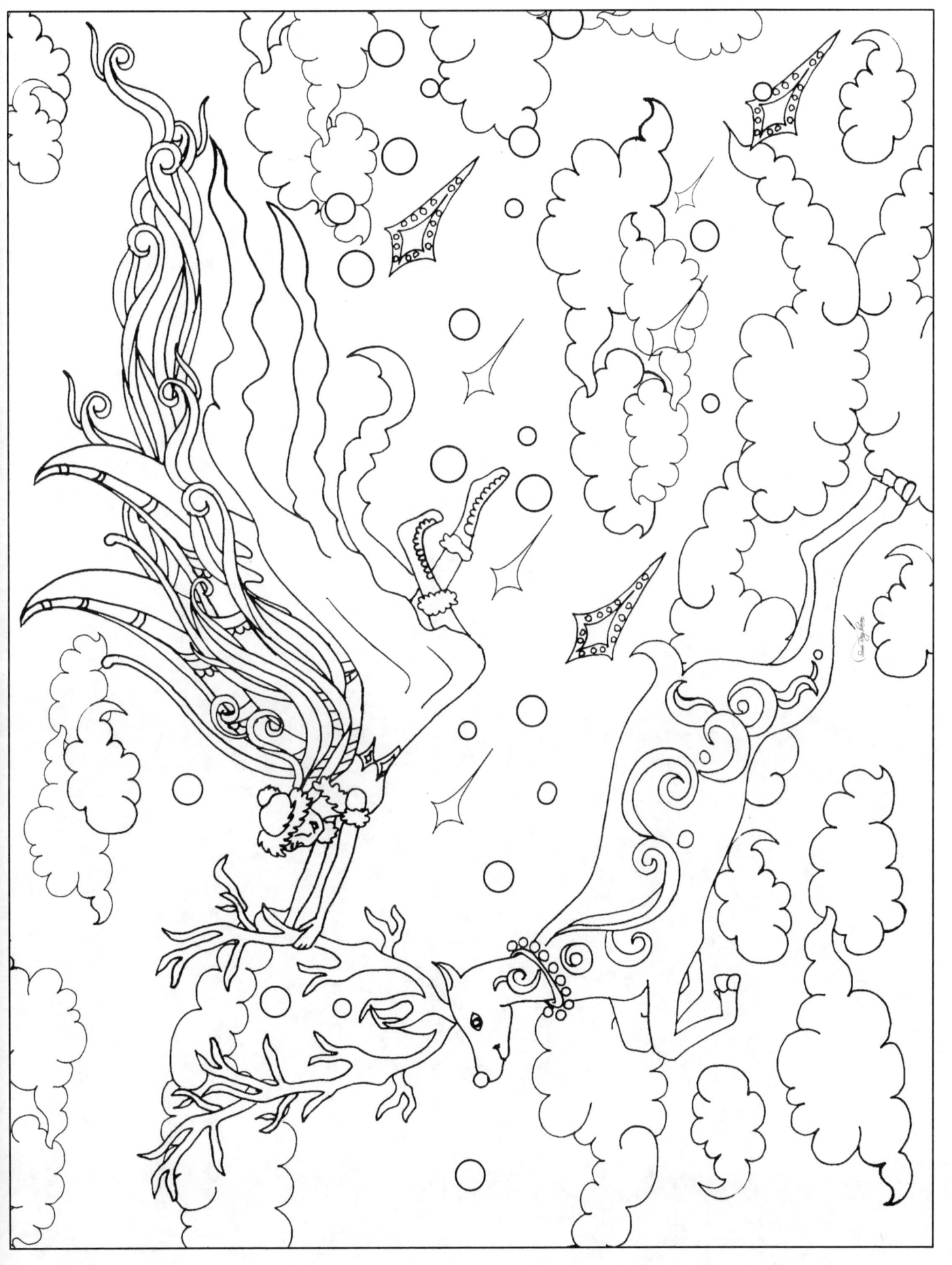

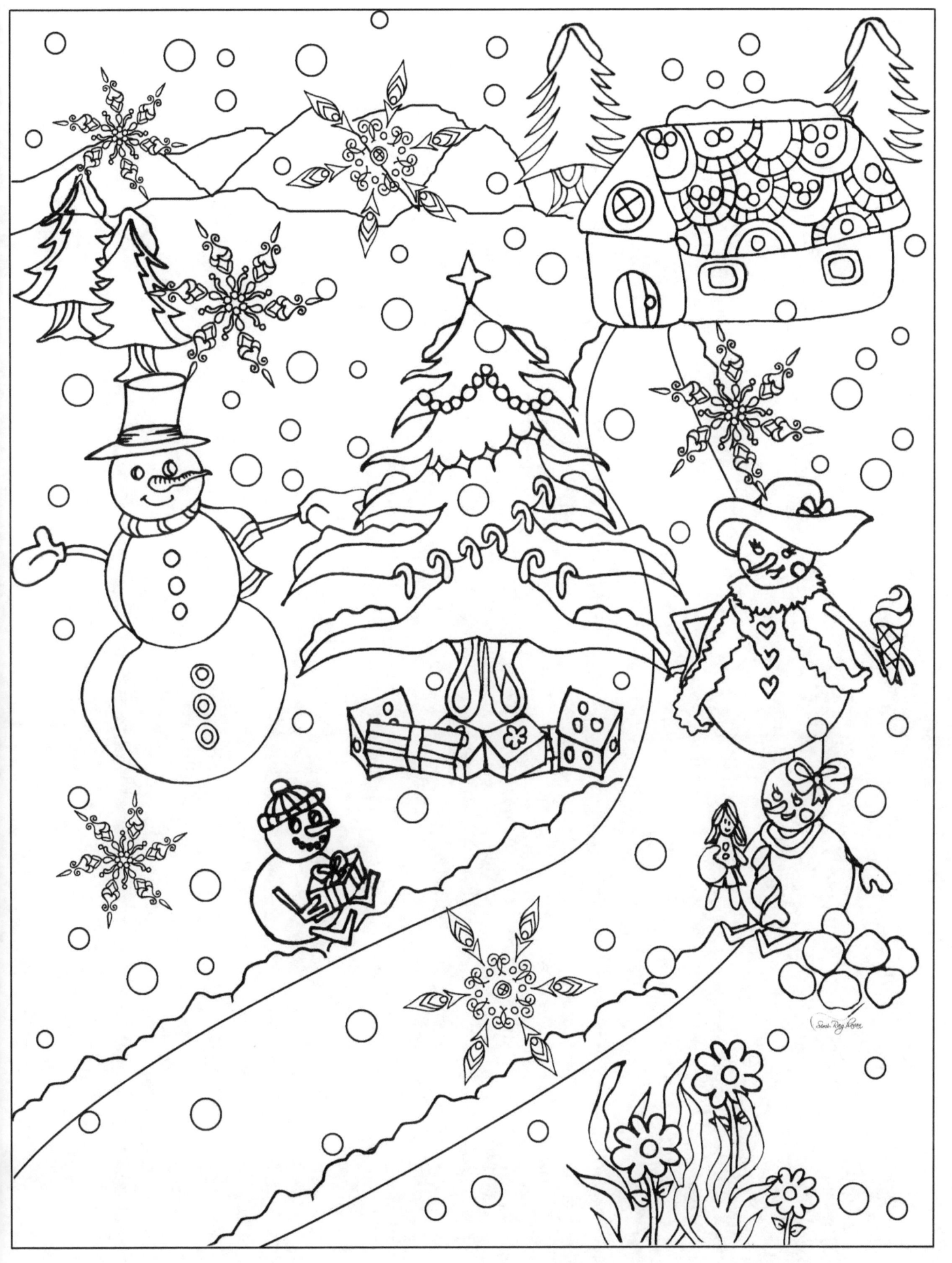

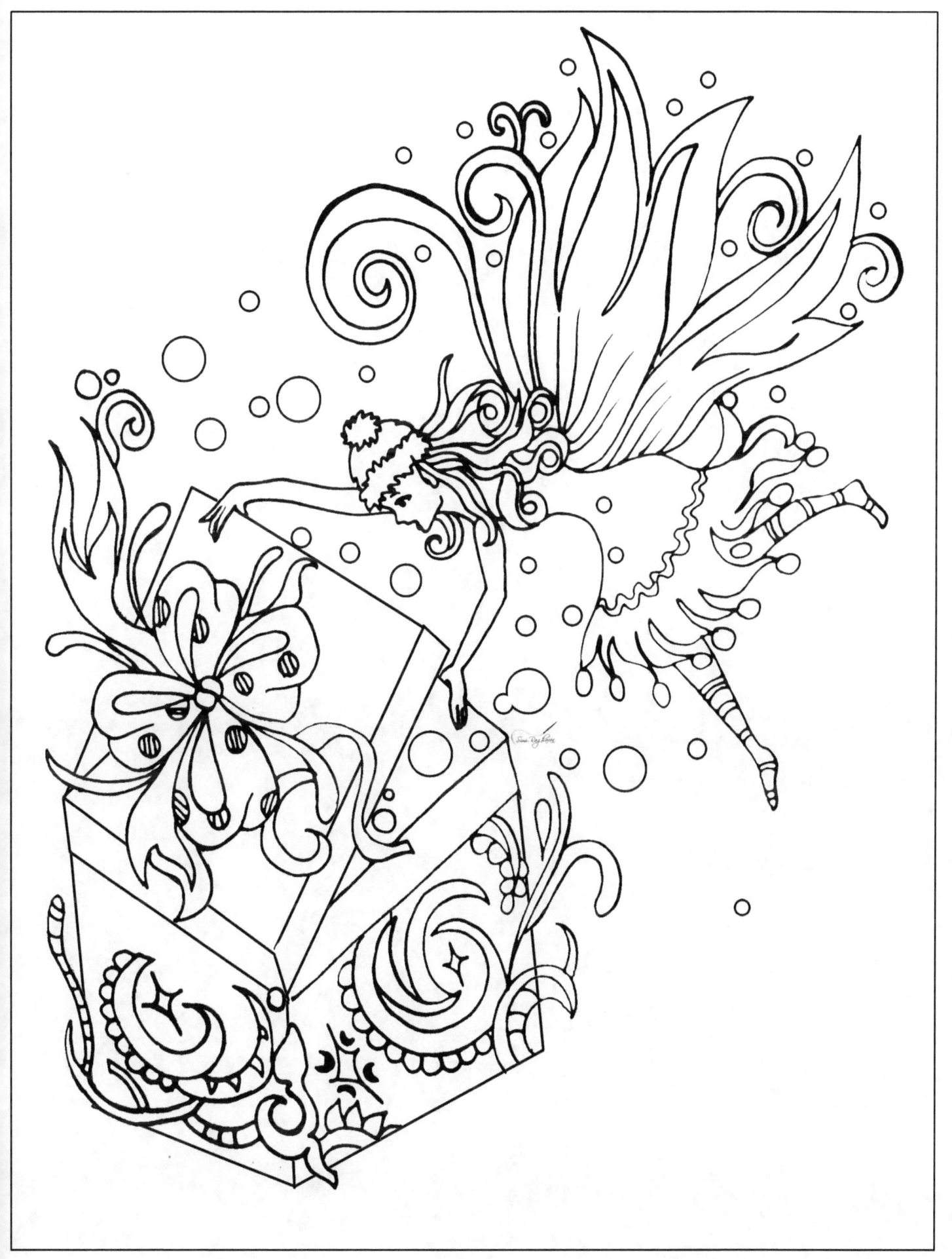

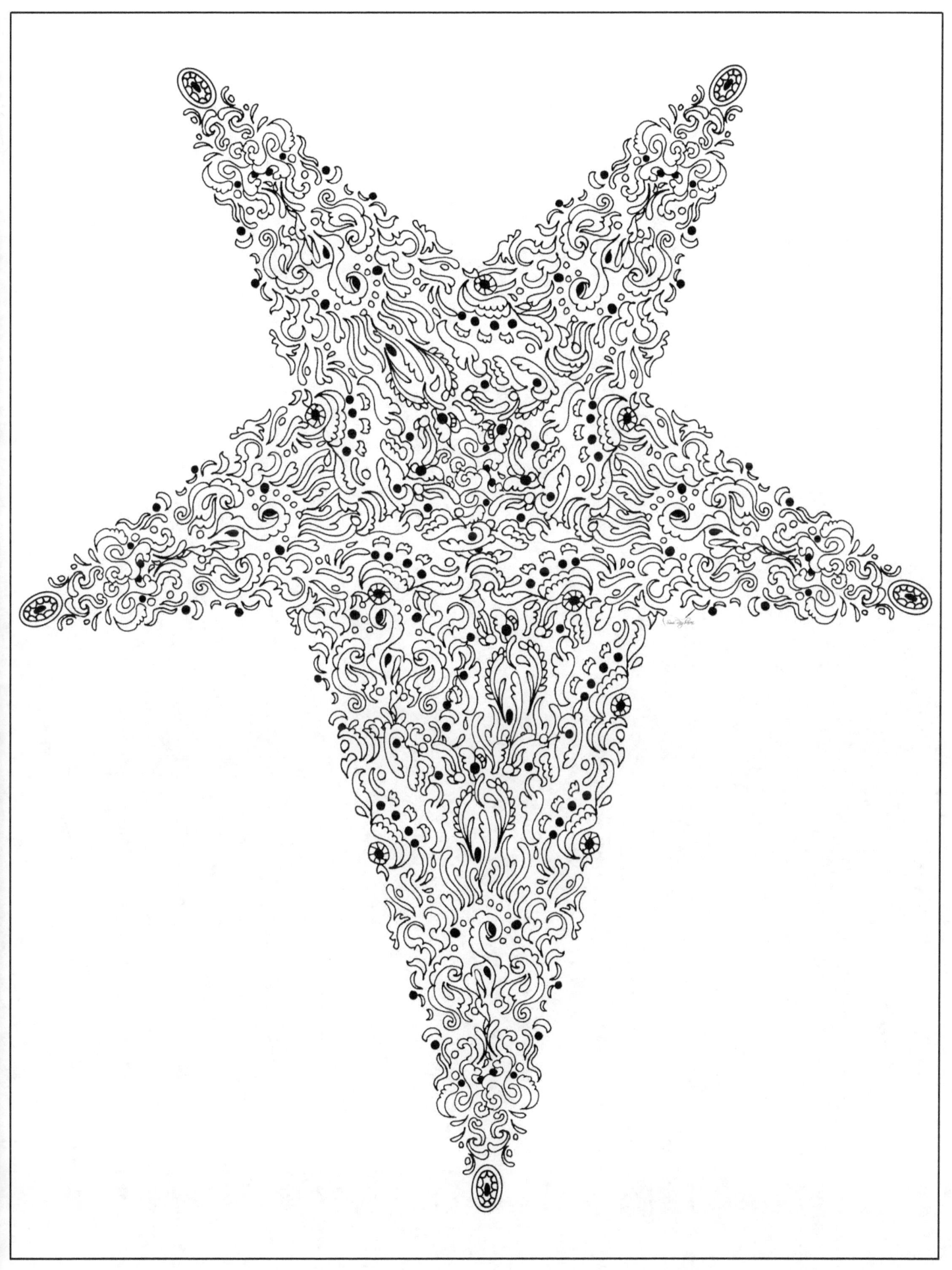

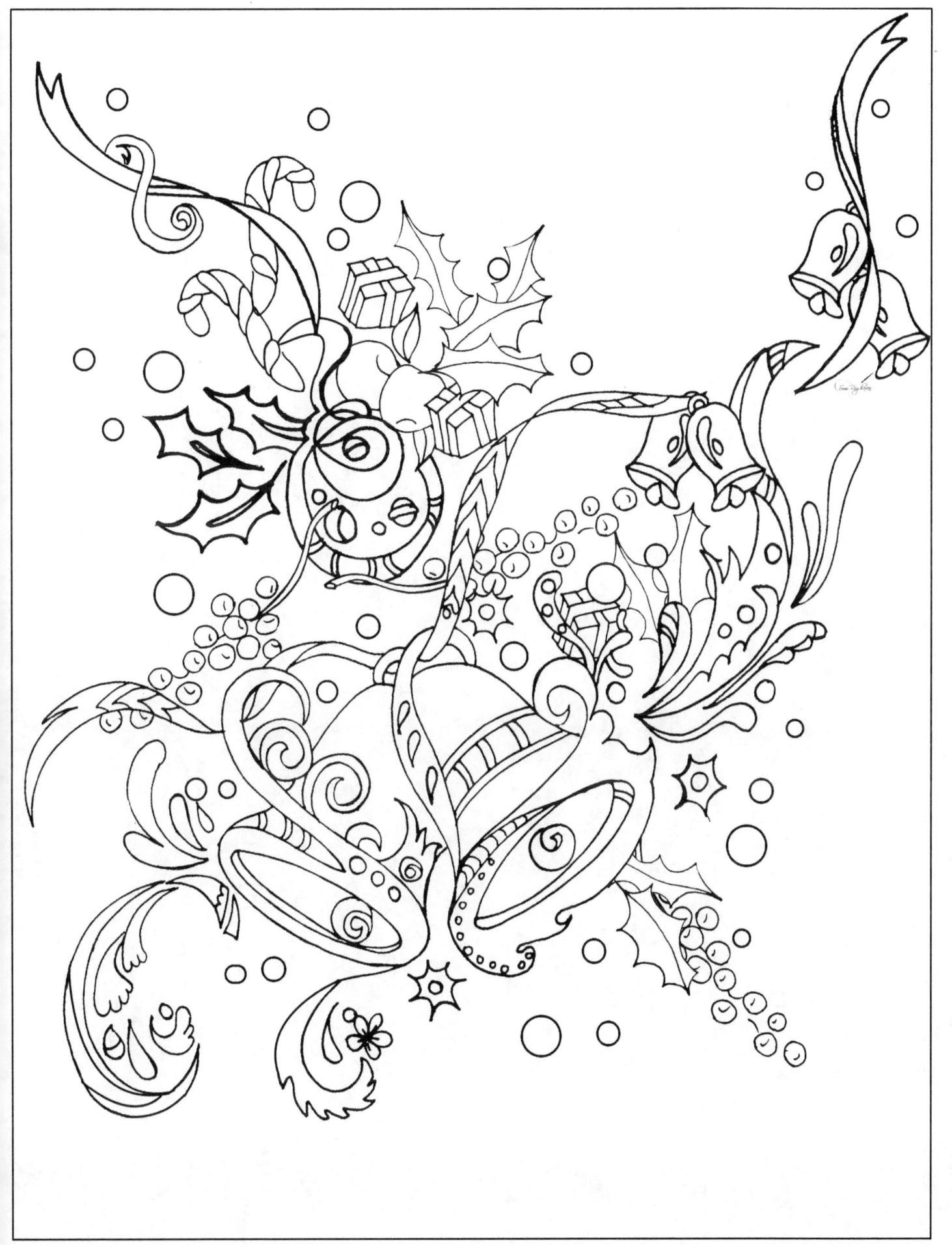

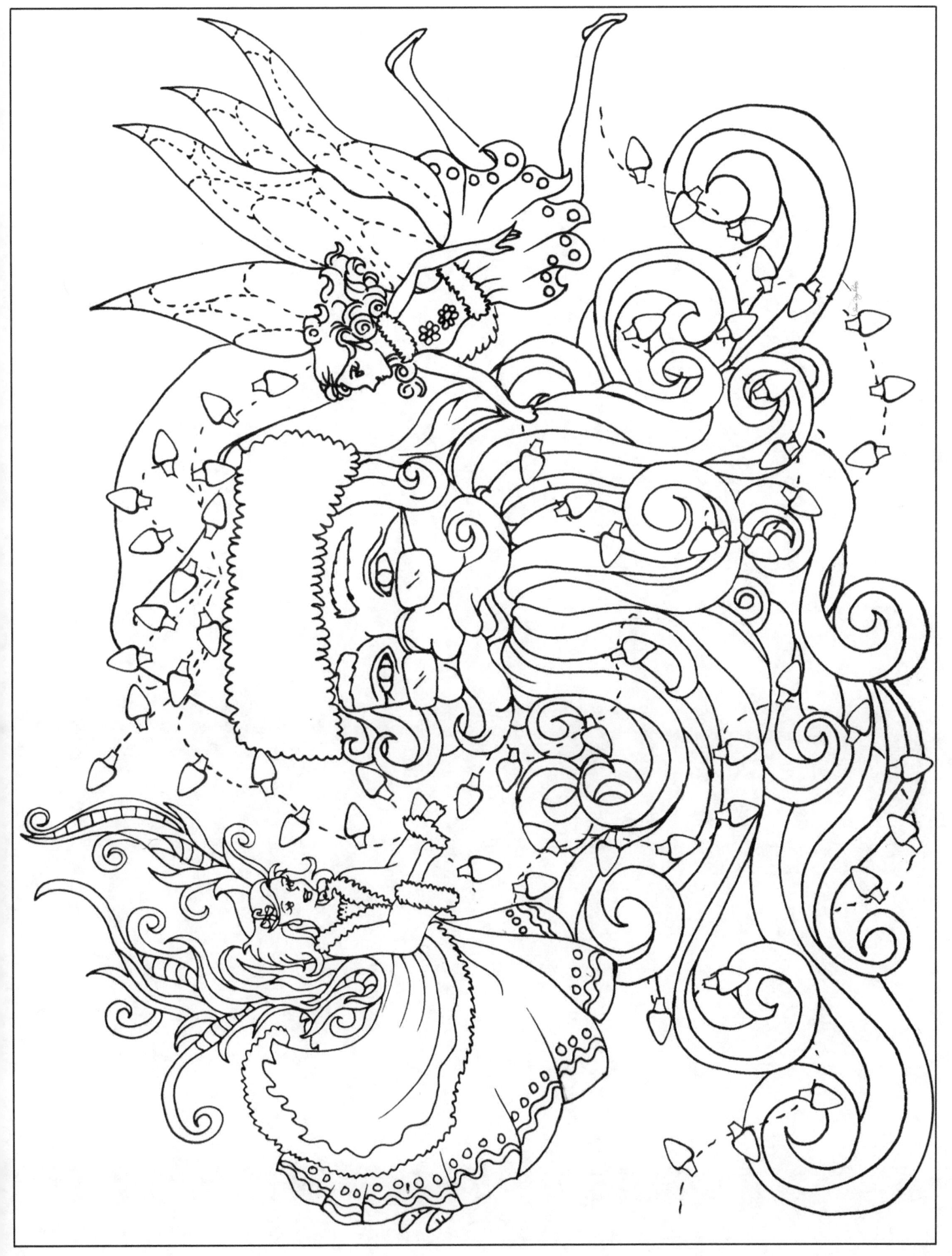

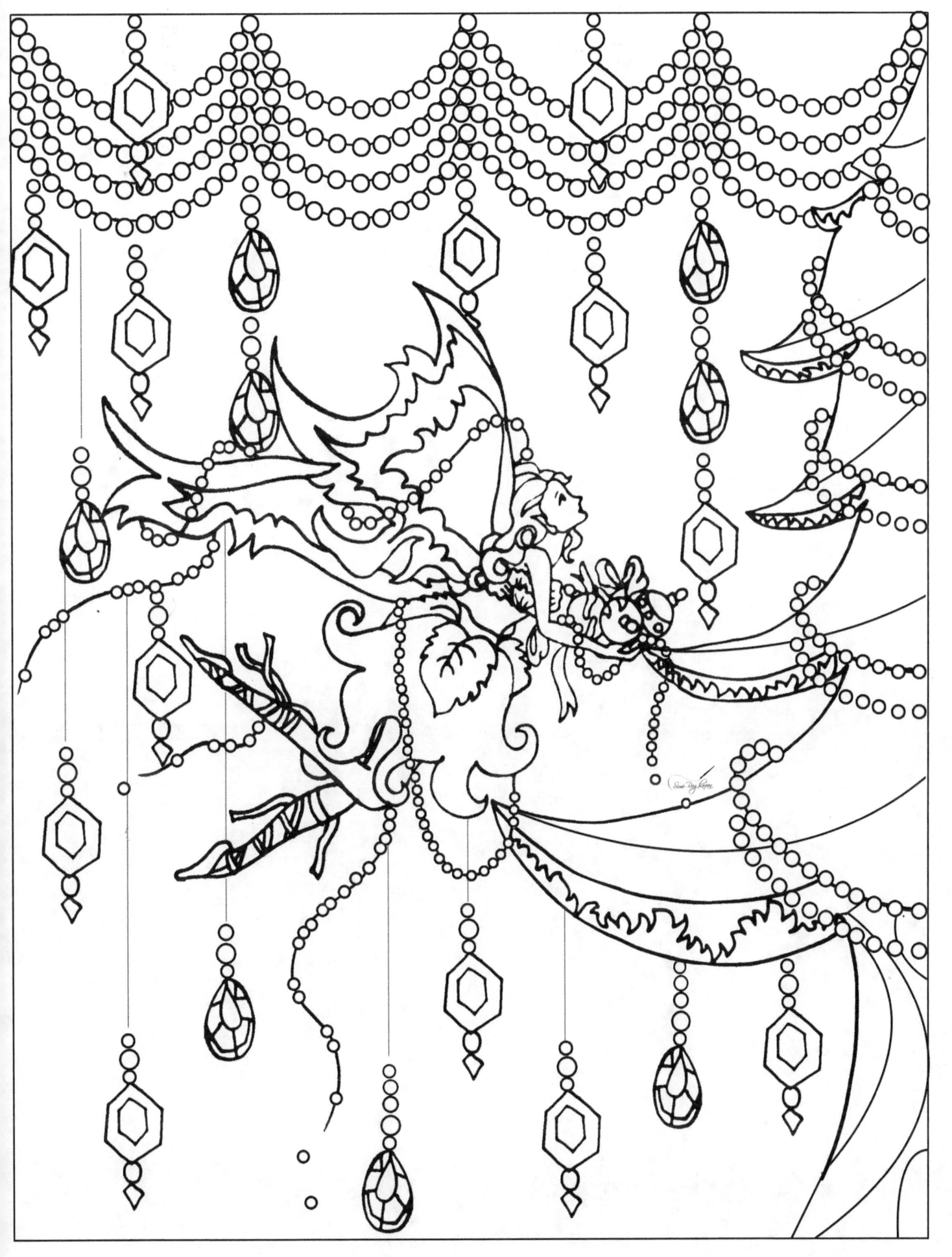

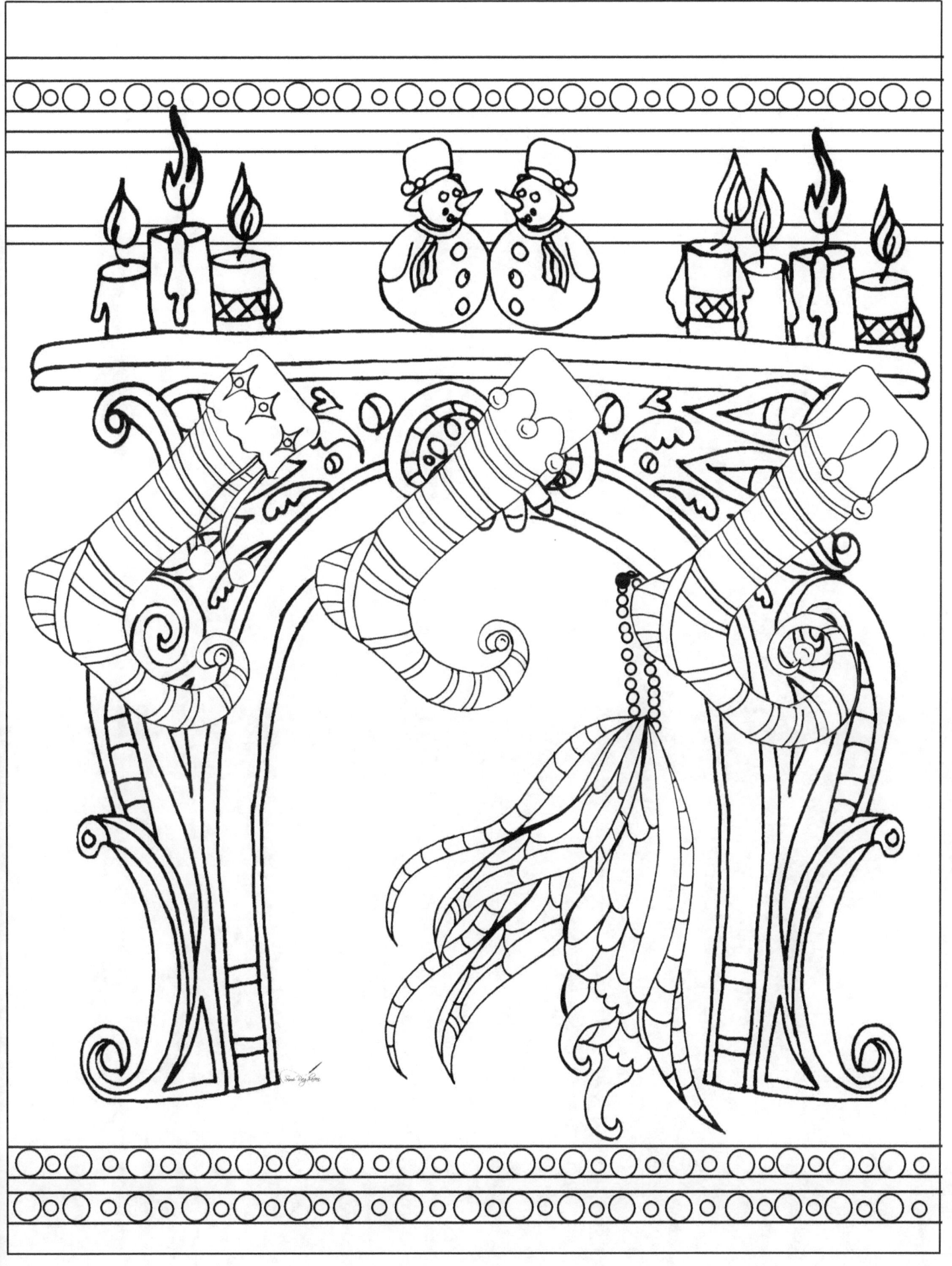

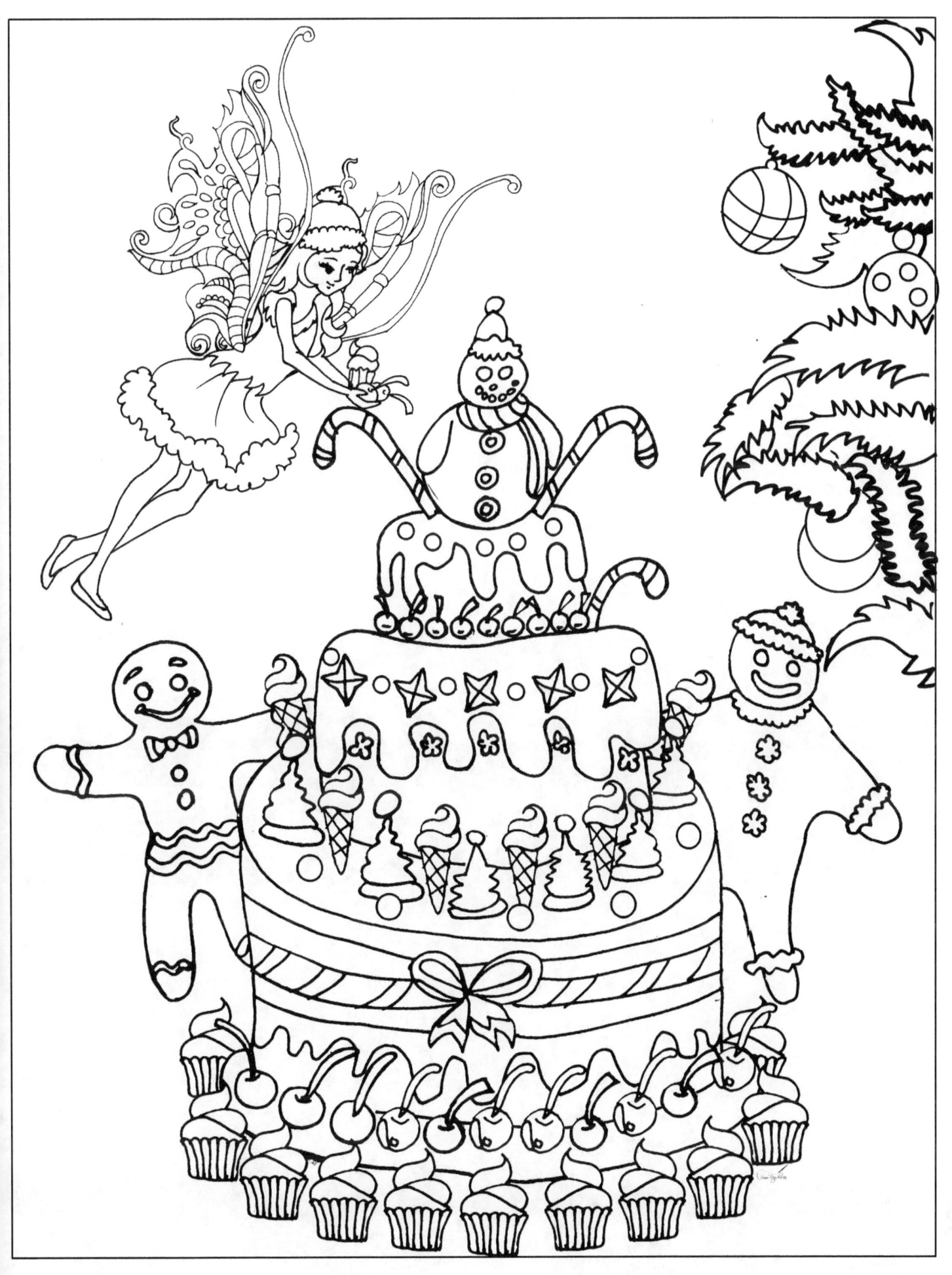

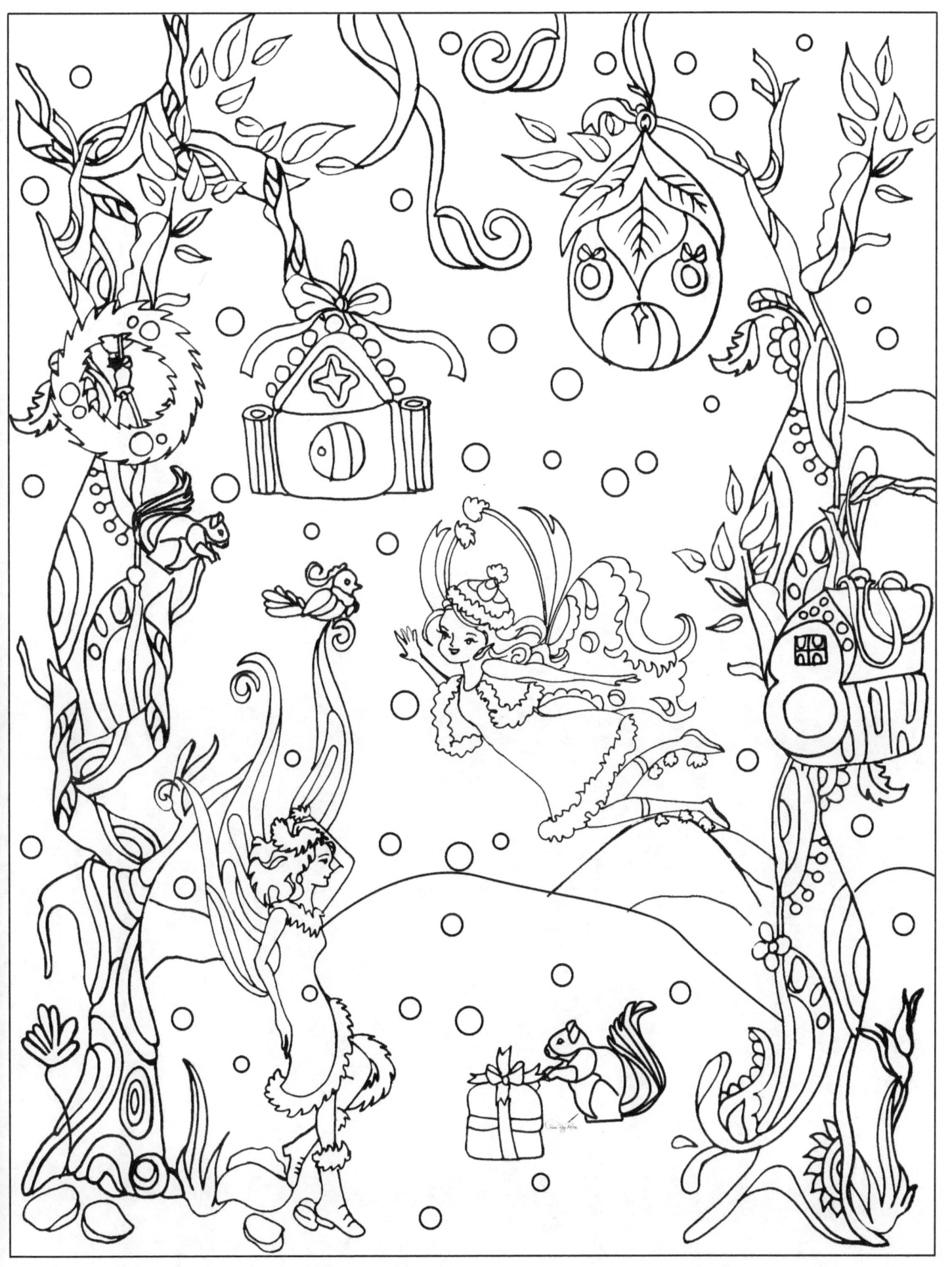

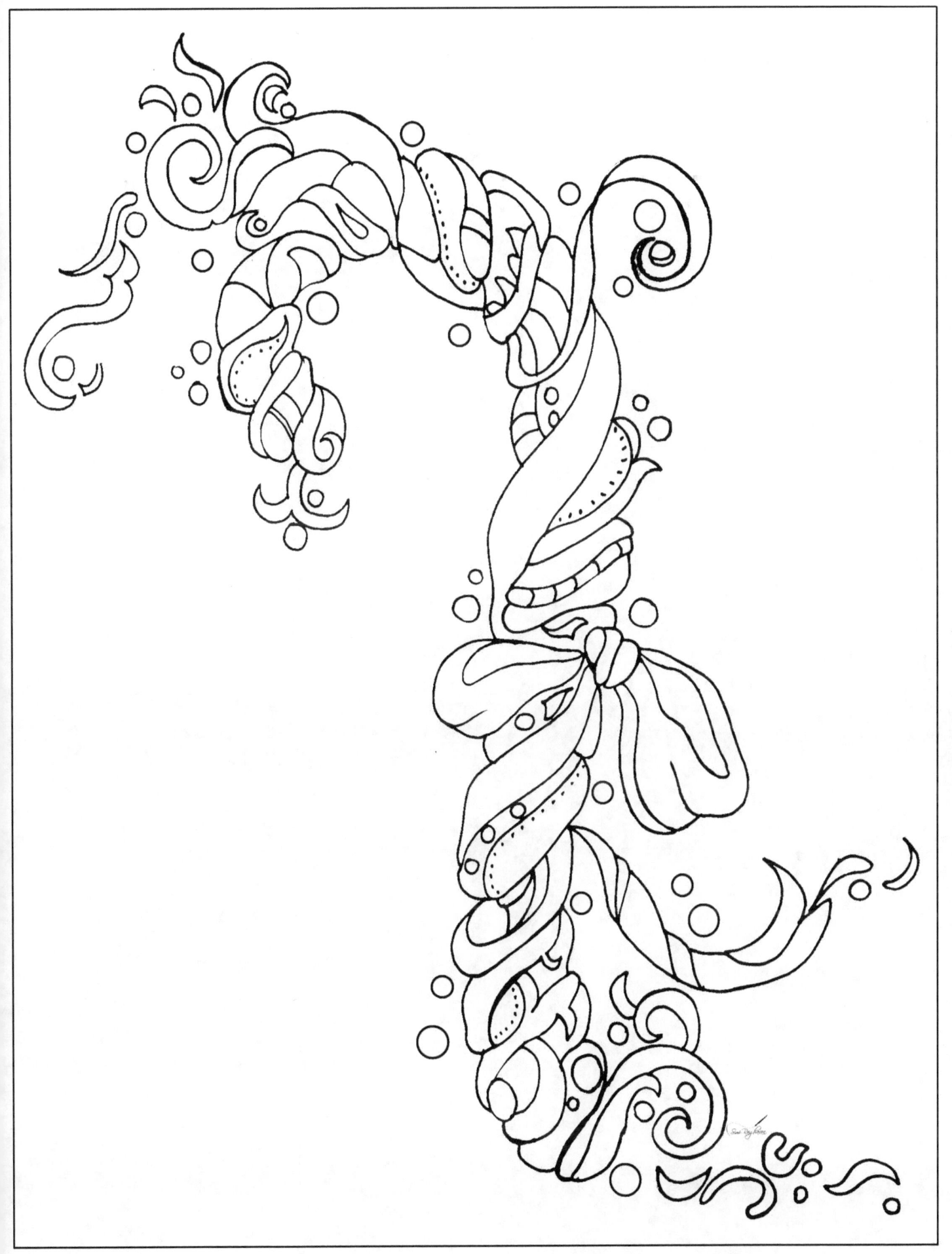

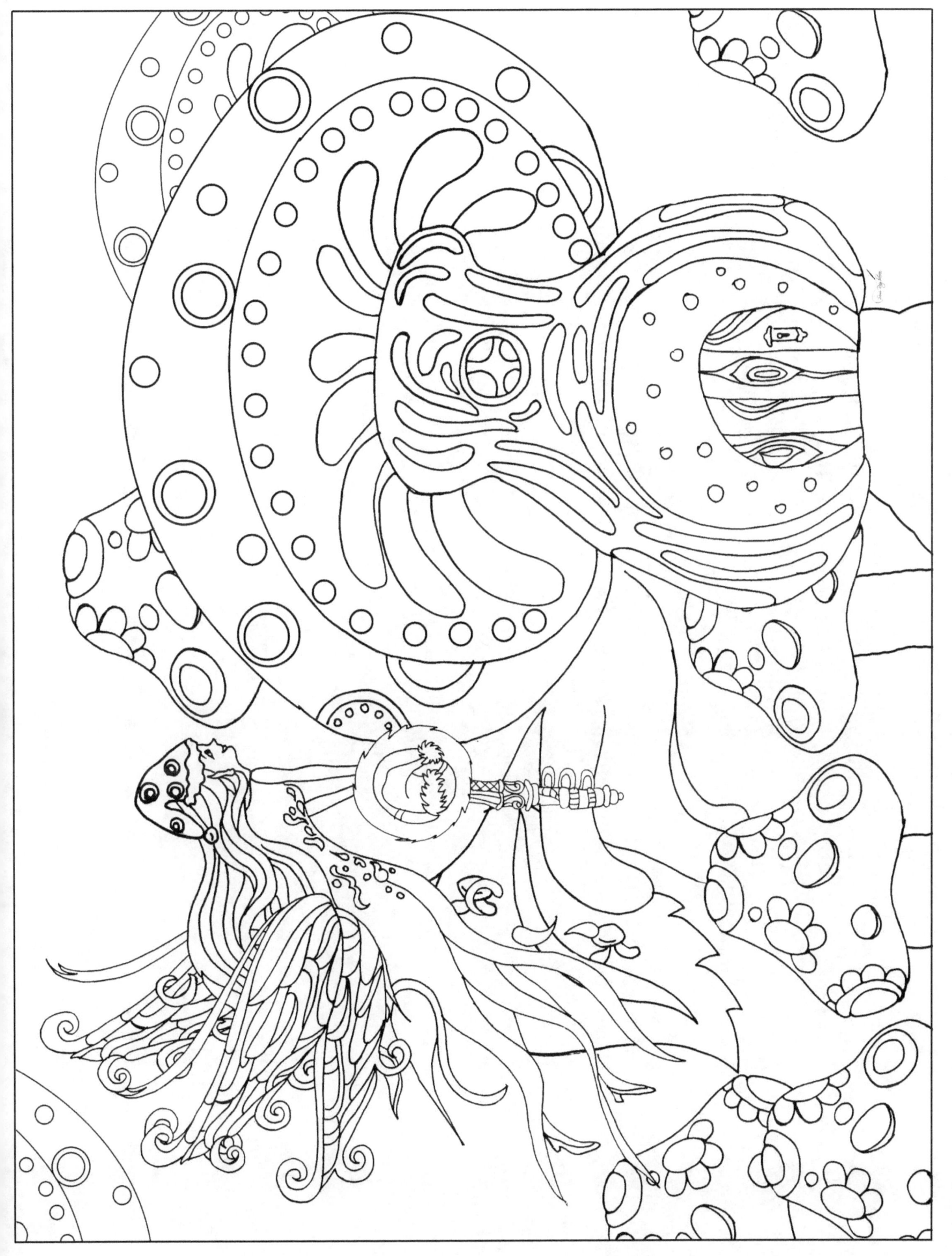

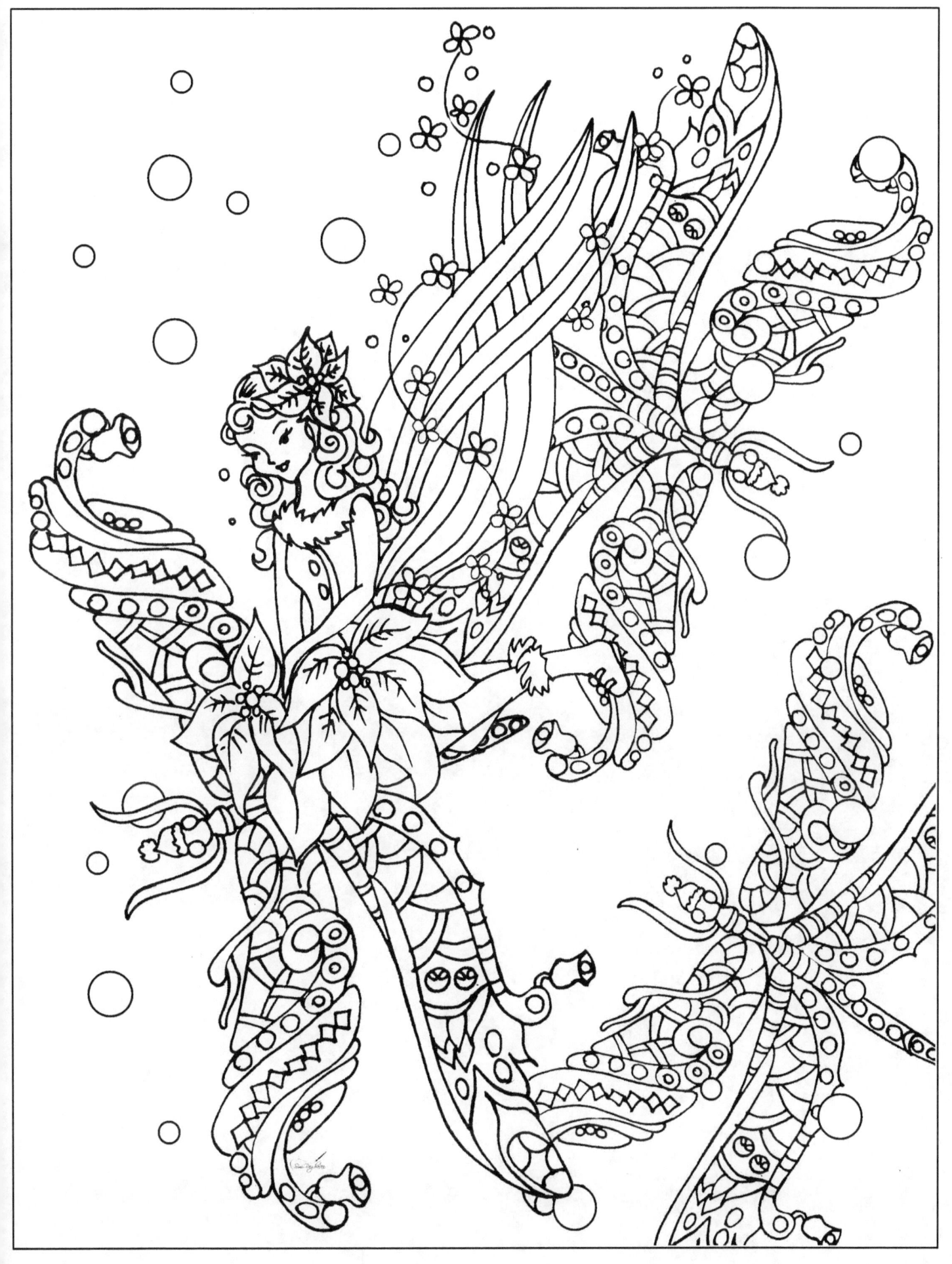

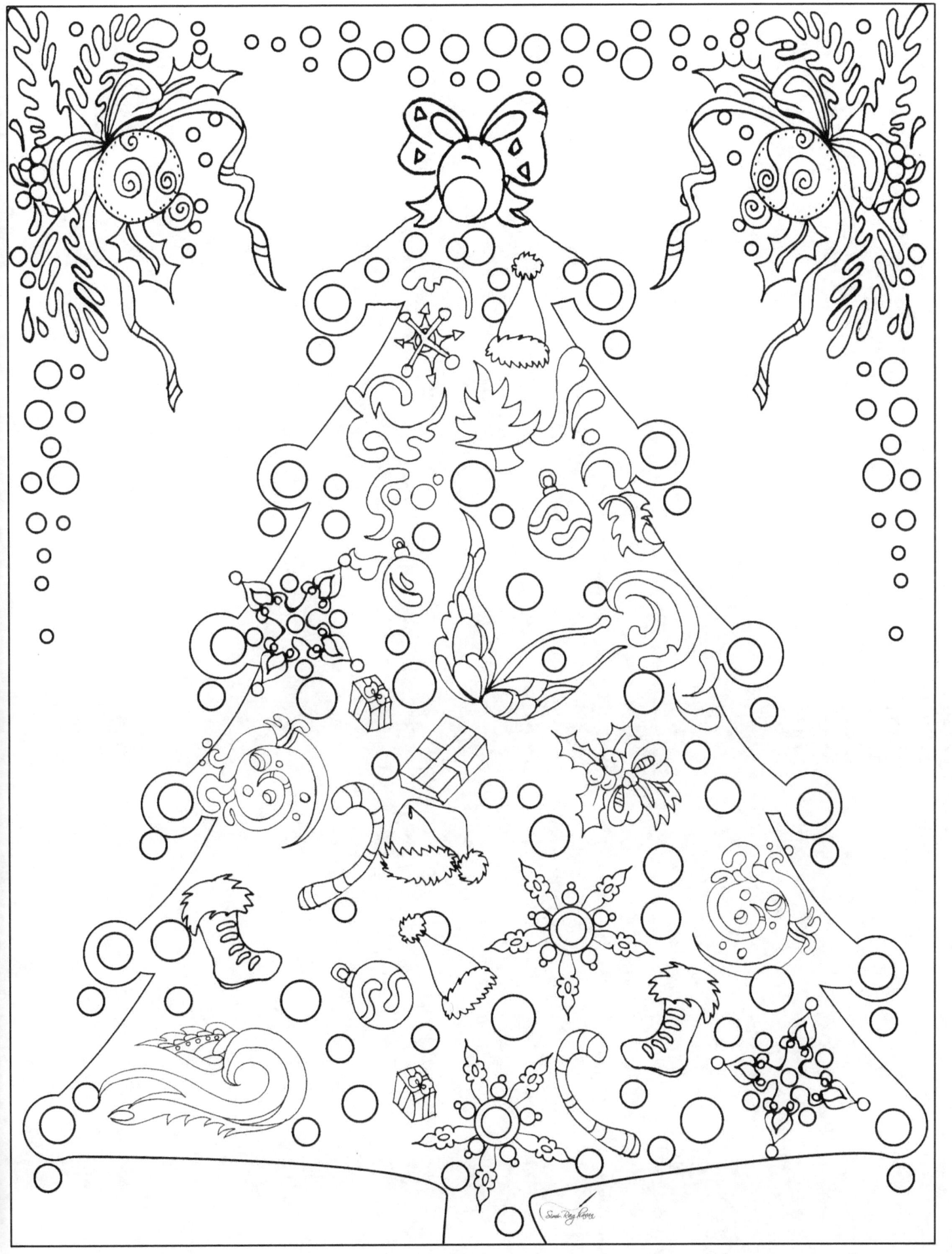

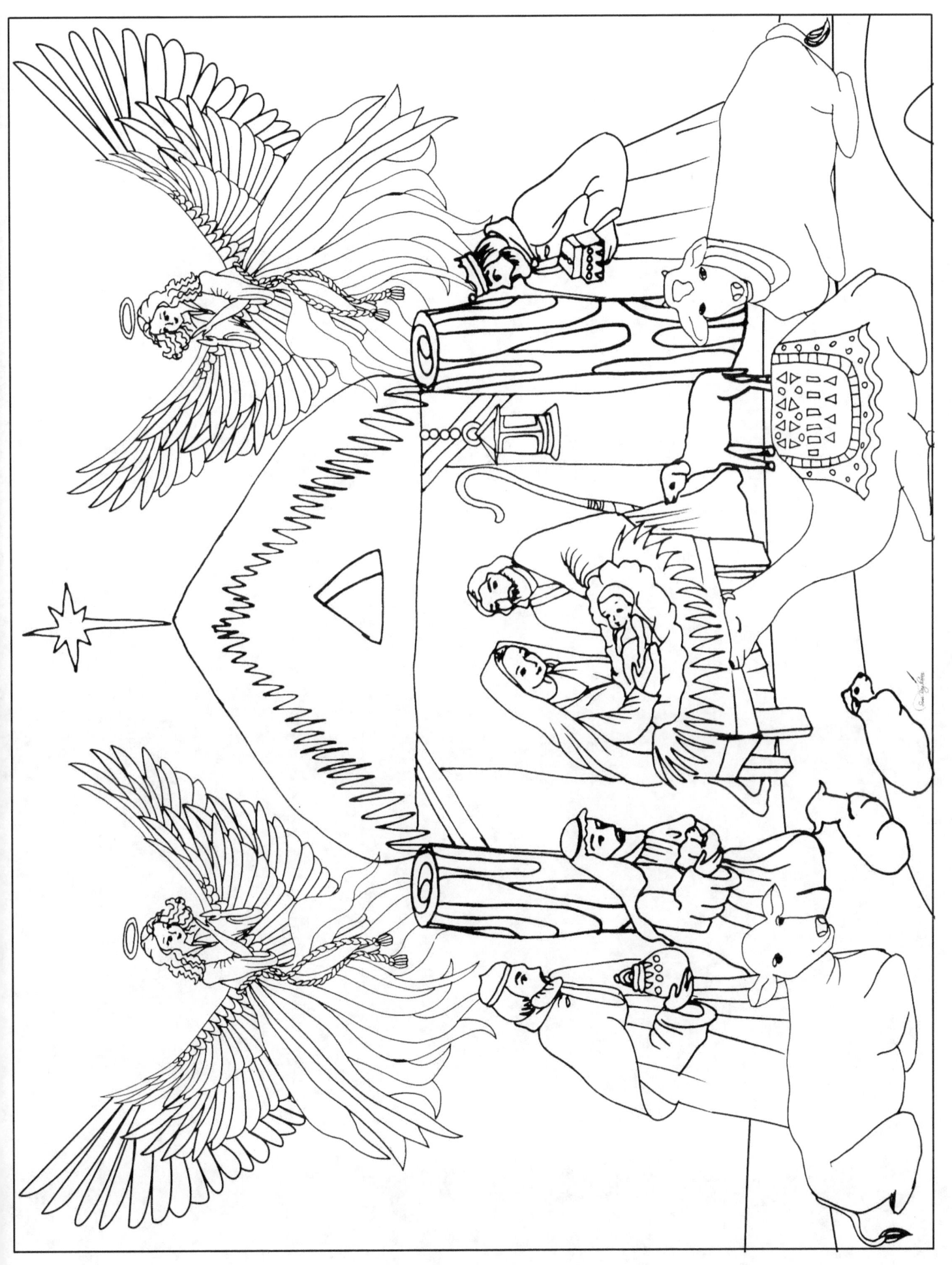

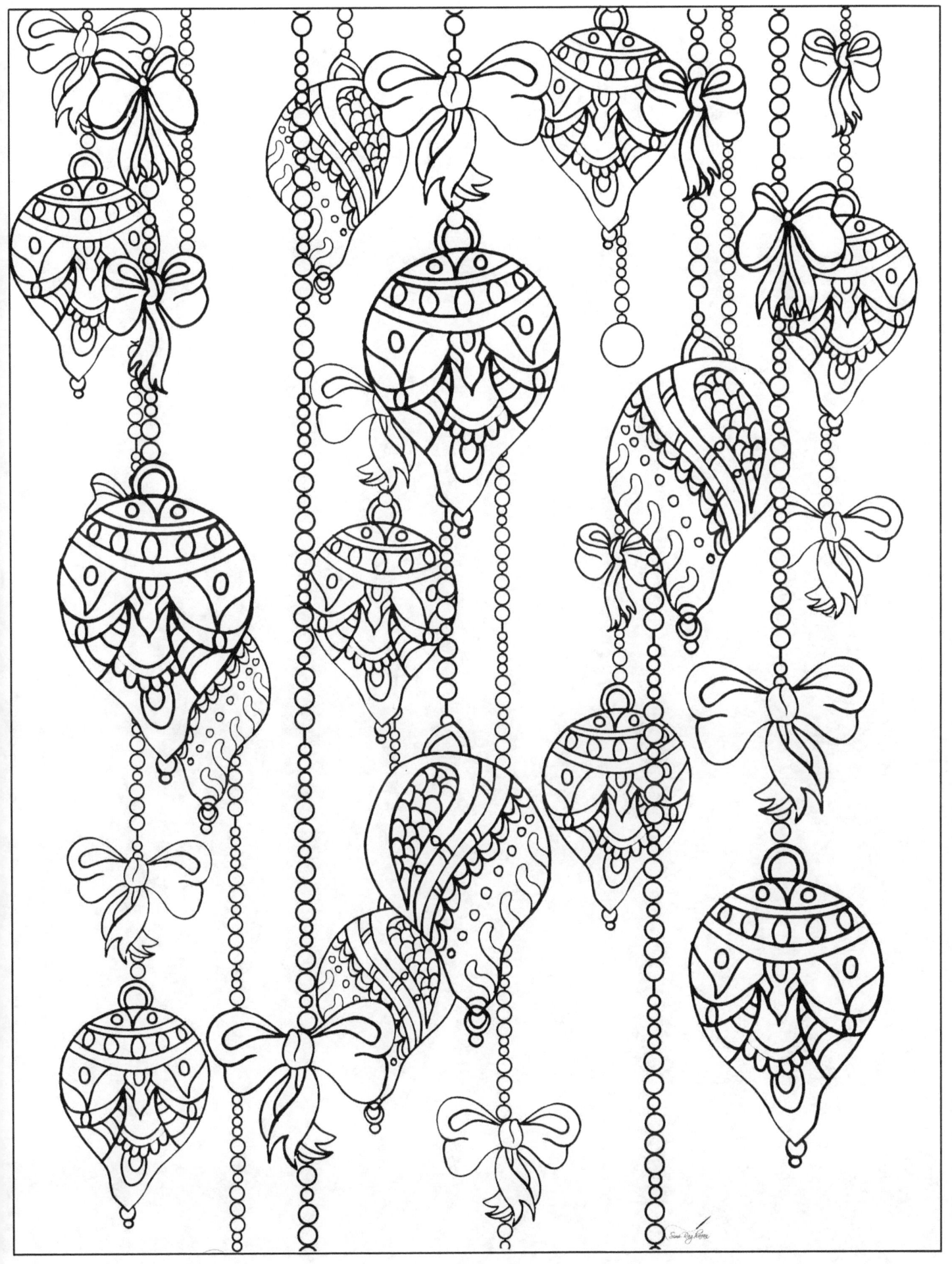

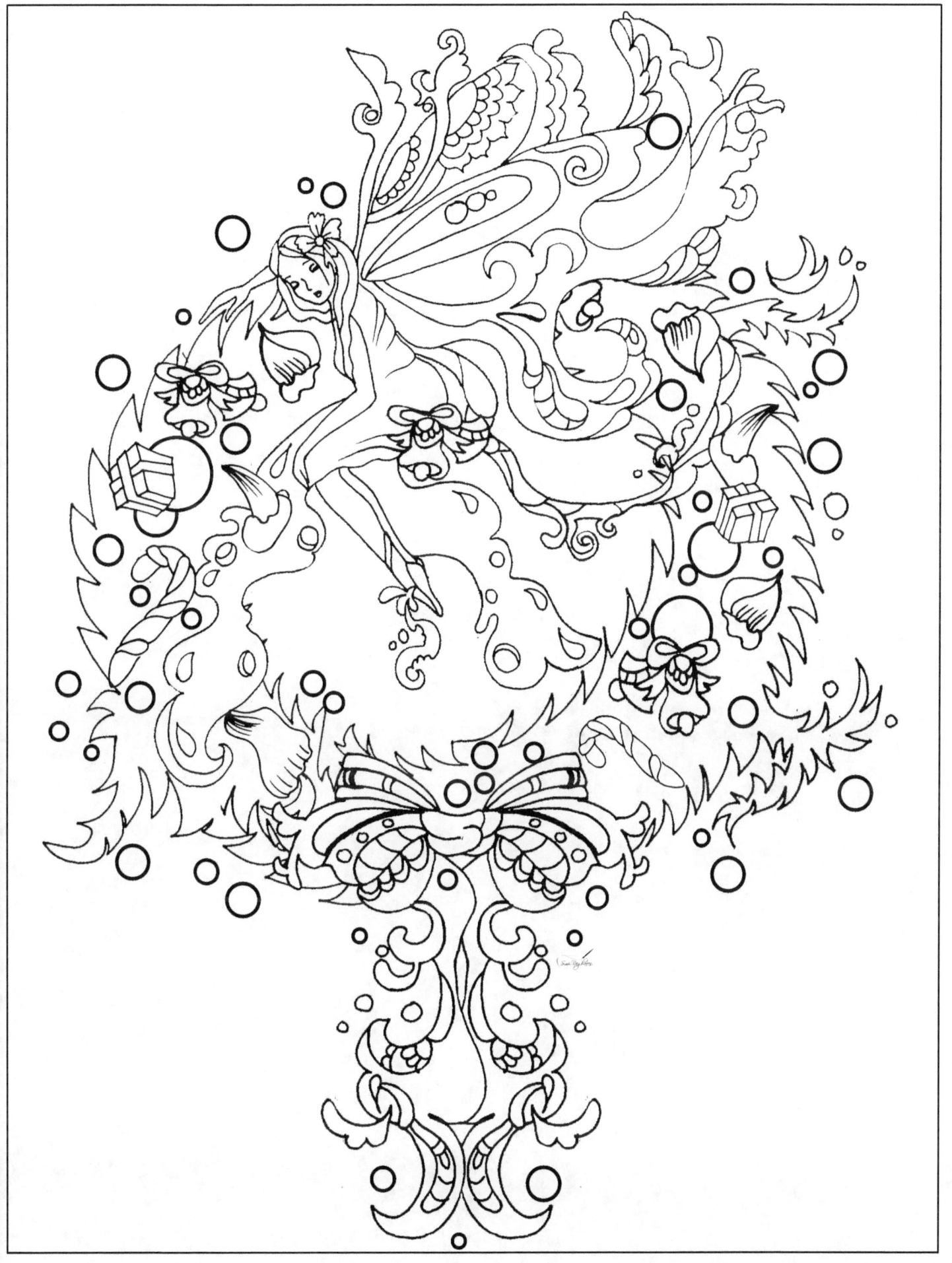

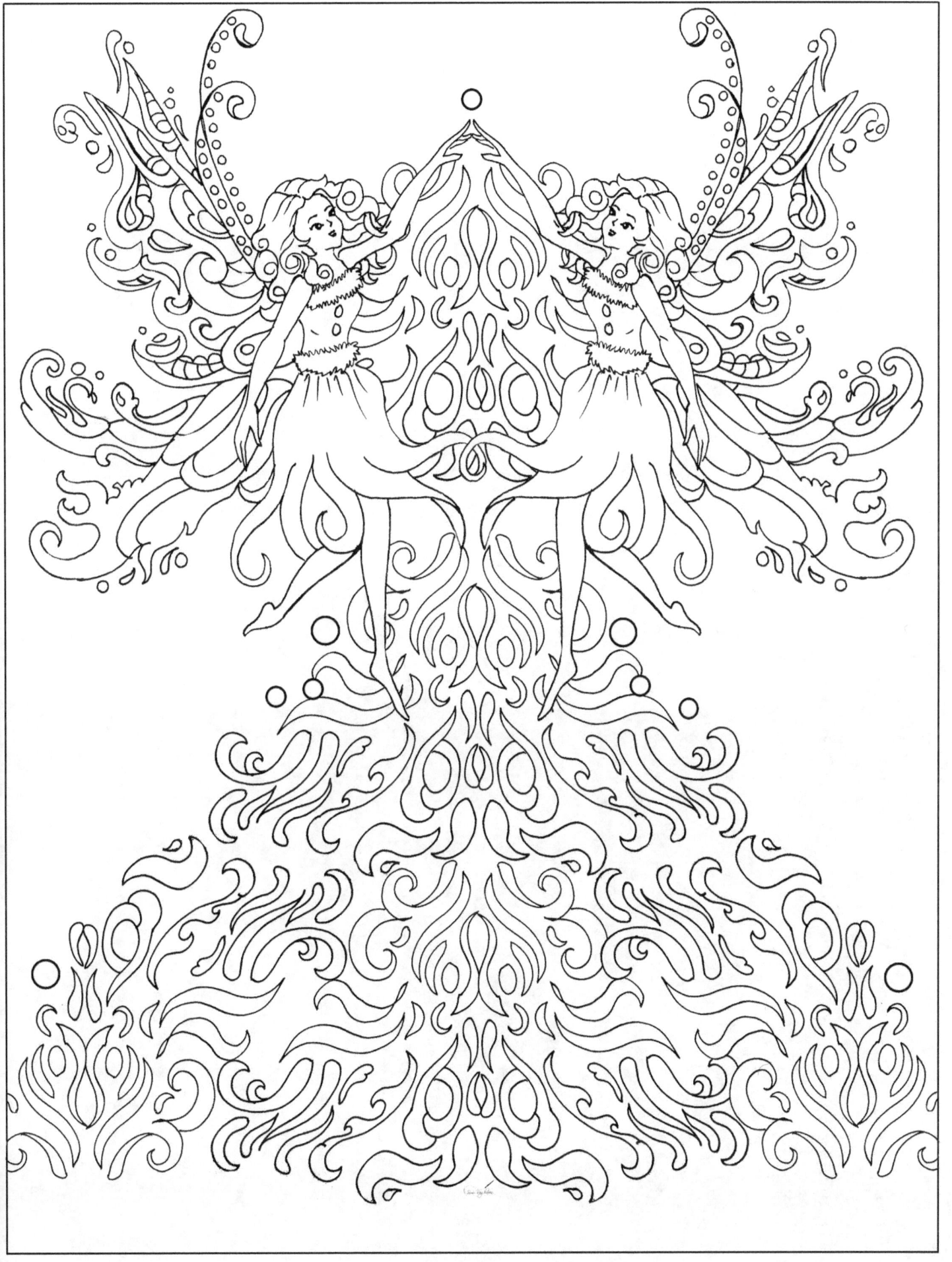

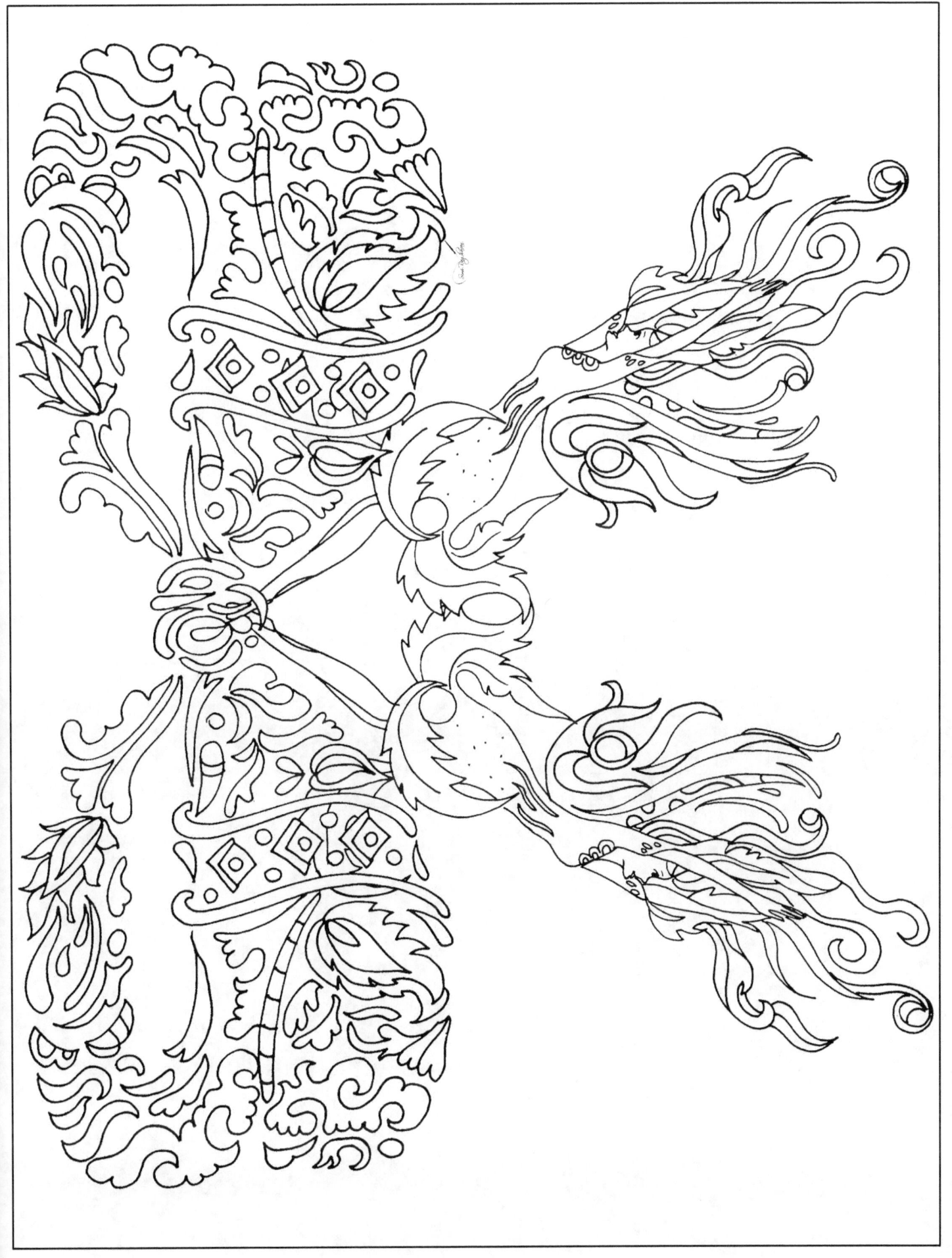

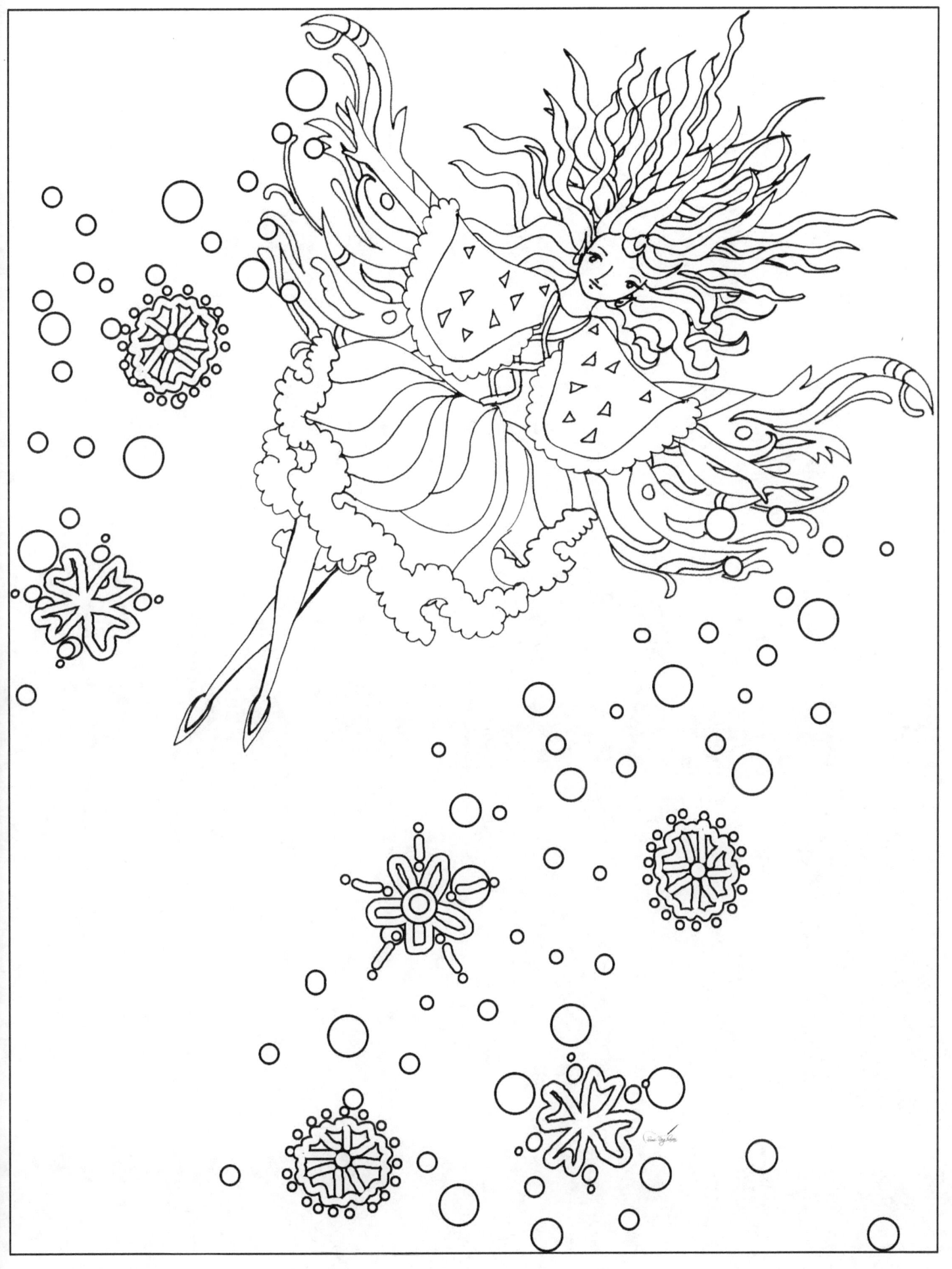

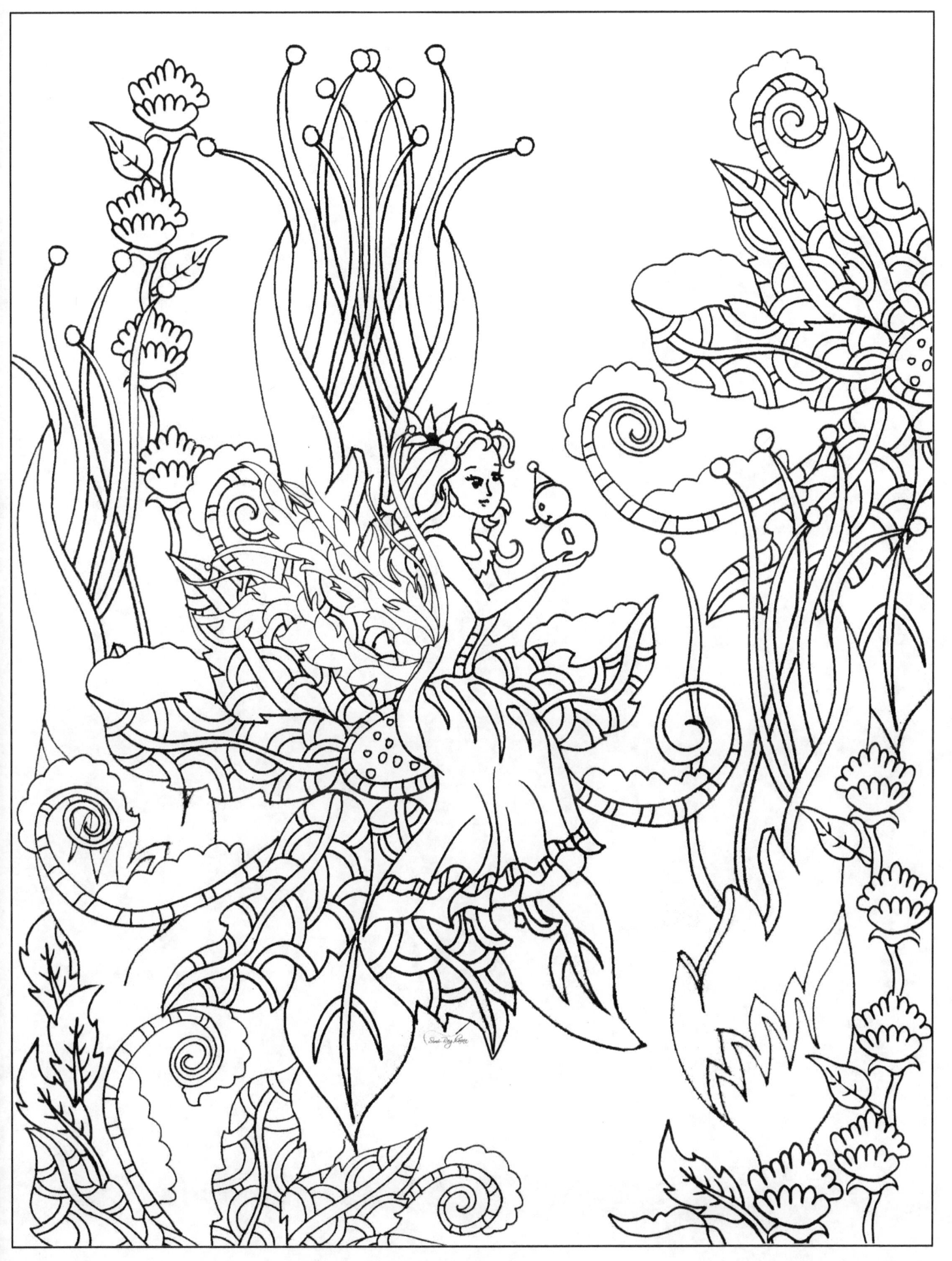